ESSENTIAL CHEMISTRY

METALS

ESSENTIAL CHEMISTRY

ESSENTIAL CHEMISTRY

METALS

JULIE McDOWELL

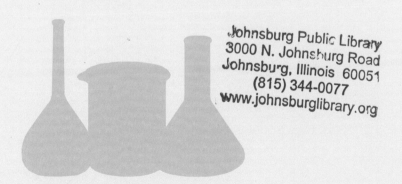

CHELSEA HOUSE
PUBLISHERS
An imprint of Infobase Publishing

METALS

Chelsea House
An imprint of Infobase Publishing
132 West 31st Street
New York NY 10001

Library of Congress Cataloging-in-Publication Data

McDowell, Julie.
 Metals / Julie McDowell.
   p. cm. — (Essential chemistry)
 Includes bibliographical references and index.
 ISBN 978-0-7910-9535-5 (sh)
 1. Metals. I. Title.

 QD171.M38 2008
 546'.3—dc22   2007049863

Chelsea House books are available at special discounts when purchased in bulk quantities for businesses, associations, institutions, or sales promotions. Please call our Special Sales Department in New York at (212) 967–8800 or (800) 322–8755.

You can find Chelsea House on the World Wide Web at http://www.chelseahouse.com

Text design by Erik Lindstrom
Cover design by Ben Peterson

Printed in the United States of America

Bang NMSG 10 9 8 7 6 5 4 3 2 1

This book is printed on acid-free paper.

All links and Web addresses were checked and verified to be correct at the time of publication. Because of the dynamic nature of the Web, some addresses and links may have changed since publication and may no longer be valid.

CONTENTS

Introducing Metals

Look around you. Right now, wherever you are reading this book—at school, at home, or outside somewhere—you are surrounded by chemical **elements** that make up not only the air we breathe and the water we drink, but also the human body and the infinite number of objects that make up our world. So far, only 111 known elements make up what is called the **periodic table**, a grid that was designed to organize the elements. Elements cannot be broken down to a simpler form by ordinary chemical or physical means, but when they are chemically combined, they form the various materials that make up our world.

About 75% of elements are classified as **metals**. Some examples of metals are gold, copper, silver, tin, iron, and aluminum. Many of them are hard and shiny, but there are exceptions. For example, sodium, which is found in table salt, is a metal, as is calcium. Both

of these metals are very soft. Another metal element, mercury, is liquid at room temperature.

Certain characteristics are common to many metals:

- *Conduction:* Metals are good conductors of electricity and are often used in electronic products such as televisions, MP3 players, and computers. Electrical cords and most cars are made up of metals. Silver and copper are two of the best conductors of electricity.
- *Reactivity:* Most metals readily combine (physically or chemically) with other substances. For example, two or more metals can combine to form a mixture known as an **alloy**. But an alloy is not the result of a chemical reaction; the result of a chemical reaction between two metals results in a **compound**. Most metals can form compounds with other elements in the periodic table. For example, sodium and potassium are two metals that are very reactive to water. When sodium reacts with water, a solution of sodium hydroxide is formed, as well as hydrogen gas. When potassium reacts with water, hydrogen gas is also formed, as well a solution of potassium hydroxide. Many metals, such as copper, zinc, and platinum, act as **catalysts** for reactions, which means that they accelerate a chemical reaction. At the end of the reaction, however, the catalyst remains, unchanged.
- *Malleability:* Most metals can be hammered or rolled into sheets, which means that they are **malleable**. Their flexibility allows them to be **ductile**, or drawn into wires. These characteristics are another reason that metals are found in electronic products, as well as objects such as eyeglass frames.

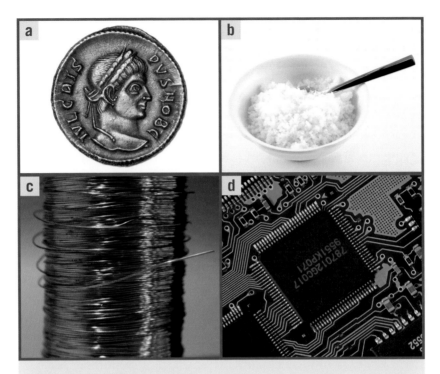

Figure 1.1   Examples of metals and their properties: (a) Coins are made from metals that have been hammered and flattened. (b) The metal sodium is highly reactive with chlorine: they chemically combine to form salt. (c) Copper is ductile and can be drawn into wire. (d) Metals are good conductors of electricity and are used in computer chips.

CHEMICAL COMPOSITION OF METALS

As mentioned, elements cannot be broken down to other, more basic components through ordinary means. Chemical elements are composed of **atoms**, which consist of three kinds of particles: **protons**, **neutrons**, and **electrons**.

Protons and neutrons are located in the atom's **nucleus**, or core. Protons carry a single, positive electric charge, whereas neutrons carry no charge. Electrons, which are much smaller than either

protons or neutrons, carry a single, negative charge. Electrons move rapidly around the nucleus in regions known as energy shells. Atoms can have multiple energy shells. Electrons in the energy shell closest to the nucleus are more tightly bound to the nucleus than electrons in shells farther away from the nucleus.

When an element is in a normal state, the number of electrons is equal to the number of protons in the nucleus. In this state, the positive charge of each proton is balanced by the negative charge of each electron. Each chemical element has distinct characteristics based on its number of protons, neutrons, and electrons. These characteristics determine how an element behaves when it combines with other elements to form compounds. The number of protons in the element's nucleus is also the element's **atomic number**. For example, hydrogen has one proton; therefore, its atomic number is 1. Sodium has 11 protons, and its atomic number is 11. The periodic table is organized by the order of each element's number of protons; that is, by each of the element's increasing atomic number.

How many electrons can occupy each energy shell? The inner-most energy shell can hold two electrons (hydrogen, in its normal state, has only one electron, which is located in the inner shell), but all other energy shells can hold a maximum number of 8 electrons.

The number of electrons in the outermost shell—the one farthest from the nucleus—is the most important to understand. These are the electrons involved in chemical bonding. The elec-trons found in the outermost energy shell are called *valence* elec-trons. Metallic elements typically have 1 to 3 electrons in their outermost energy shell. By comparison, nonmetals usually have 5 to 8 electrons in their outermost energy shell.

Because metallic elements have few valence electrons, they can easily lose their electrons to other atoms that can readily accept electrons. Nonmetals have more valence electrons than metals. They readily accept electrons to complete their outermost energy shells.

When an atom either loses or gains an electron, it develops an electrical charge and is then called an **ion**. Ions are able to conduct

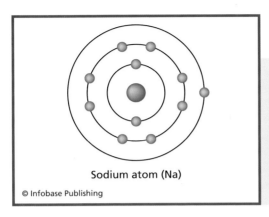

Sodium atom (Na)

© Infobase Publishing

Figure 1.2 A sodium atom has 11 electrons: two in the innermost shell, eight in the next shell, and one in the outermost shell.

electricity. When an atom gains electrons, it becomes negatively charged and is called an **anion**. When an atom loses electrons, it is positively charged and is called a **cation**.

An **ionic bond** is formed when two ions with opposite charges join together. Ionic bonds are particularly strong. One example of an ionic compound is table salt (sodium chloride), which is formed by the reaction between the metallic element sodium (Na) and the nonmetal chlorine (Cl).

THE PERIODIC TABLE OF THE ELEMENTS

Ninety-one of the 111 elements in the periodic table occur in nature. The remaining 20 elements are synthetic, which means they can only be made in a laboratory. All chemical elements are organized in a chart called the periodic table of the elements. In this table, the elements are located in specific places in a chart according to their properties and behaviors. The element's name and each element's symbol, which is usually made up of one or two letters, are listed. The one-letter symbol is always written with an uppercase letter, such as *F* for fluorine and *N* for nitrogen. When the element has a two-letter symbol, the first letter is uppercase and the second is lowercase, such as *Al* for aluminum and *Si* for silicon. In the periodic table in the appendix, note where the metals are located; their squares are light purple.

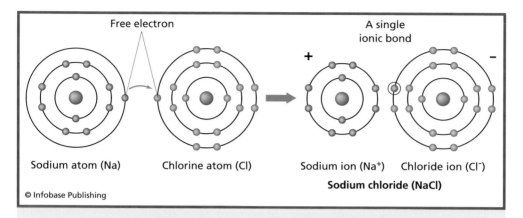

Free electron

A single
ionic bond

+   −

Sodium atom (Na)   Chlorine atom (Cl)   Sodium ion (Na⁺)   Chloride ion (Cl⁻)

Sodium chloride (NaCl)

© Infobase Publishing

Figure 1.3   Sodium and chlorine combine to form table salt (NaCl). The sodium atom (Na) loses its outermost electron and becomes a cation (Na⁺). The chlorine atom gains an electron and becomes an anion (Cl⁻).

The periodic table is made up of rows (known as periods) and columns (known as groups). The elements listed in each period have the same number of electron shells. Elements in the top row—hydrogen (H) and helium (He)—have one shell, whereas every element in the second row, or period, has two shells. The elements of the third row, or period, have three shells and so forth. The last row in the periodic table has 7 energy shells.

Elements located in the same group, or column, exhibit similar chemical behaviors. For example, sodium (Na) and potassium (K) are in the same group: when each of these elements is dropped in water, it reacts violently and can even produce an explosion. Elements in groups exhibit similar behaviors because they have the same number of electrons in their outermost energy shells (valence electrons). Every element in the first column, known as Group 1, has one electron in its outermost energy shell, whereas every element in the second column, Group 2, has two electrons in the outermost energy shell. As the groups increase in numbers from left to right—not including the **transition metals**—so do the number of valence electrons. Elements in the last column have eight electrons in their outermost energy shell.

THE FATHER OF THE PERIODIC TABLE: DMITRI MENDELEYEV (1834–1907)

A professor of chemistry at the University of St. Petersburg in Russia, Mendeleyev developed the periodic table around 1869 for inclusion in a chemistry textbook for his students. As part of his research, he listed each element on cards, including their properties. When he examined these cards, he noticed that if the elements were arranged according to their mass, common properties appeared in sections. He built a table by organizing the elements into horizontal rows based on their mass, with each row's lightest element listed at the left end of that row and the heaviest listed at the right. Ordering one row after another, Mendeleyev also arranged elements with similar properties into vertical columns.

Figure 1.4   Russian chemist Dimitri Mendeleyev invented the periodic table of elements in 1869. The scientist left gaps in the table, correctly hypothesizing that new elements would be discovered.

When Mendeleyev developed this initial table, he left gaps for elements that he believed existed but had not yet been discovered. He turned out to be correct: by leaving room for these undiscovered elements within the row and column organization, he was able to accurately predict their properties. But there are important differences between the modern periodic table and Mendeleyev's initial version. When Mendeleyev was alive, none of the elements in the column that contains helium and radon had been discovered, so this group—Group 18—is relatively new to the modern table. In addition, Mendeleyev's table lists some of the atomic masses out of order. In order to have this early table come out right, Mendeleyev had to sometimes place elements with greater masses ahead of those with smaller masses. However, knowledge of the atom advanced greatly in the twentieth century, and the appropriate way to order chemical elements was determined to be by atomic number (the number of protons), rather than by atomic mass. The modern periodic table organizes elements according to atomic number.

In the periodic table, special metals are located in Groups 1 and 2. Group 1 metals are the most reactive to compounds such as air and water; Group 2 metals are slightly less reactive to these and

GREAT SCIENTISTS: SIR HUMPHREY DAVY

Born in Cornwall, England, Sir Humphrey Davy (1778–1829) was a pioneer in the discovery of many metals. Initially educated as a pharmacist (known during this time in history as an *apothecary*), Davy was fascinated by science and chemistry and liked to experiment with light and heat.

In 1800, the world's first battery was invented by Alessandro Volta (1745–1827). Volta's invention made it possible to separate water (H_2O) into its two basic elements—oxygen and hydrogen—through a process known as electrolysis. The invention of the battery allowed Davy to isolate sodium and potassium electrically, and he later isolated strontium, barium, magnesium, and boron.

Figure 1.5   Sir Humphrey Davy devised a way to protect iron from corroding.

One of Davy's most important areas of research had to do with corrosion, which is the gradual change that metals, especially iron and copper, undergo when they are exposed to water and air. Corrosion leads to the formation of rust, which causes the metal to crumble. Iron is a primary element in many structures, including buildings and ships. Davy discovered how corrosion was destroying ships, particularly those of the British Royal Navy. He developed methods of combining metals that would protect and preserve important structures, like ships, against the effects of corrosion.

other compounds. Group 1 metals are called **alkali metals**. Group 2 metals are called **alkaline earth metals**. The transition metals are located in Groups 3 through 12. Below the transition metals, and extracted from period 6, are the **lanthanide series**, or rare earth metals. The row below that, extracted from period 7, are the **actinide series**, or **radioactive** metals.

There are some exceptions to the patterns of the periodic table, such as those found within the transition metals. In addition, the elements in the first period, hydrogen (H) and helium (He), also have unique characteristics. For example, hydrogen is special because it can both lose and gain an electron and thus has characteristics of both Groups 1 and 7. In the case of helium, it has only two electrons in its outermost shell, even though it is grouped with elements that have eight electrons in their outermost shells.

SUMMARY

The periodic table is made up of elements—most of which are classified as metals. Elements are composed of atoms, which consist of three kinds of particles—protons, neutrons, and electrons. There are three characteristics common to most metals. Many metals are good electricity conductors, many are reactive with other elements on the periodic table, and most metals are malleable, meaning they are flexible.

Alkali Metals

The alkali metals—lithium, sodium, potassium, rubidium, cesium, and francium—make up Group 1 of the periodic table. These metals are highly reactive. For example, if potassium is dropped into water, the reaction will transform potassium into potassium hydroxide and hydrogen gas. When these metals react with water, hydrogen gas is given off, and heat—often hot enough to create flames—can appear. The heat produced by the interaction is enough to liquefy the metal.

All alkali metals are reactive, and their reactivity increases with their atomic number, or as you move from the top to the bottom of the group in the periodic table. This increase in reactivity involves the electron in the outermost shell, which gets farther away from the nucleus as you move down the metals in Group 1. The farther away this electron is from the nucleus, the less tightly it is bound to the atom. The looser this bond, the more likely the

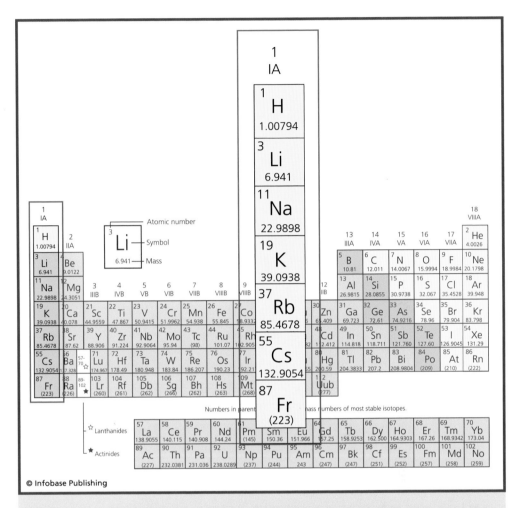

Figure 2.1   The alkali metals are found in Group 1 of the periodic table. The alkali metals consist of lithium, sodium, potassium, rubidium, cesium, and francium.

electron is to detach from the atom in a chemical reaction. For instance, when cesium (near the bottom of the group) reacts with water, it results in an explosion, whereas when lithium (at the top of the group) reacts with water, the result may be nothing more than some fizzing and the appearance of bubbles on the surface.

Two of the alkali metals, sodium and potassium, are some of the most common elements on earth. Yet, like the other alkali

metals, they were not discovered until relatively recently. Because water is so abundant and easily obtained, most scientists use it to conduct their experiments, but because alkali metals are so reactive with water, it took a while for scientists to isolate these elements.

This chapter looks at various aspects of each of the alkali metals. (Notice that hydrogen's location on the periodic table makes it appear as if it belongs in Group 1 with the rest of the alkali metals, even though it is actually classified as a nonmetal.) The history and other characteristics of each of these metals will be discussed. Many of the alkali metals play important roles in the environment, in technology, and in health and medicine.

POTASSIUM

Potassium was the first alkali metal to be identified. It was discovered in 1807 by Sir Humphrey Davy (1778–1829) when he noticed the tiny molten globules that formed after he had passed an electrical current through some molten potash, a compound containing potassium and other elements such as oxygen and hydrogen. This was the first time an alkali metal had been isolated, and Davy named it *potassium* after the potash compound from which he isolated it.

Potassium has a silvery and white appearance and is very soft. Because potassium is so reactive with water, it is never found in a pure state in nature, but its compounds are abundant in seawater and silicate materials, such as plant fertilizer. In nature, plants absorb potassium chloride (KCl) through the soil. Some potassium stays in the soil, combining with other elements. It is dissolved in streams and rivers, eventually making its way to seawater.

Potassium plays a key role in many important compounds in our world. For example, potassium interacts with pure oxygen to produce potassium **superoxide** (KO_2), which is used to make breathing devices like those that are used by firefighters and mine rescue workers. The potassium superoxide used in the devices reacts with exhaled carbon dioxide (CO_2) and water to produce oxygen, allowing people to breathe.

Another important compound is potassium hydroxide (KOH), which is used in certain types of batteries and in the manufacture of liquid soap, in addition to other products. Potassium nitrate (KNO_3) is also an important compound with many uses. Also known as saltpeter, KNO_3 looks like ordinary table salt, but it most definitely should not be eaten. Saltpeter is a preservative and also a key component of fertilizer. Potassium nitrate is also commonly used as an explosive. Gunpowder, for example, consists of potassium nitrate, wood charcoal, and sulfur. Heating gunpowder releases a large amount of nitrogen gas, along with carbon dioxide. The sudden release of these gases causes an explosion. Another compound, potassium chlorate ($KClO_3$), is also an explosive that is used to make matches and fireworks.

Potassium is also famous for one of its **isotopes**, radioactive potassium-40, which has a long **half-life** of 1.25 billion years. (Half-life refers to the amount of time it takes for half of the element's atoms to disintegrate.) Potassium-40 occurs naturally and is used by researchers to determine the age of rocks. As potassium-40 decays, it becomes a **noble gas** called *argon*. By determining how much argon is present in a rock, researchers can estimate the rock's age. Using this technique, scientists have estimated some rocks on Earth to be as old as 3.8 billion years.

SODIUM

Sodium was the next alkali metal to be discovered after potassium. Sir Humphrey Davy isolated sodium in 1807 (around the same time he identified potassium) by running an electric current through molten caustic soda, or soda ash, to produce sodium hydroxide.

Sodium is a bright, silvery metal that is soft and has a low **density**. Like potassium and the other alkali metals, it is too reactive—especially with water—to be found as a pure element in nature. Nevertheless, sodium is the sixth most abundant element in the Earth's crust, and its compounds play a vital role in nature. For example, seawater is a natural source of salt (NaCl). When water

evaporates from the seawater, salt beds are formed. Over time, these salt beds accumulate and can be mined much the same way that coal is removed from underground mines. Salt comes in many varieties. Rock salt, for example, comes from **mineral** deposits and sea salt comes from the evaporation of seawater. Both of these salts must first be refined by being dissolved in fresh water. The water in the solution then evaporates and the salt is recrystallized. This recrystallized product is essentially table salt, which is sold in food markets and used to flavor food.

Sodium hydroxide (NaOH) is one of the most important compounds used by industry. It is produced by the **electrolysis** of sodium chloride in water. This compound is a strong cleaning agent that is used to make products such as drain and oven cleaners. Sodium hydroxide is an excellent grease remover because it reacts with fatty substances to create a new substance that dissolves in water. Another common compound is sodium bicarbonate ($NaHCO_3$), also known as baking soda. Baking soda has numerous uses, such as for the production of baked goods, where it helps dough rise. It is also used as an antacid to help neutralize excessive stomach acid. Sodium bicarbonate is also used in fire extinguishers where the compound is mixed with an acid to generate carbon dioxide, which is then used to extinguish flames.

TABLE 2.1: ALKALI METALS: BOILING POINTS AND MELTING POINTS		
ALKALI METAL (CHEMICAL SYMBOL)	BOILING POINT	MELTING POINT
Lithium (Li)	2448°F (1342°C)	358°F (81°C)
Sodium (Na)	1621°F (883°C)	208°F (98°C)
Potassium (K)	1398°F (759°C)	147°F (64°C)
Cesium (Cs)	1240°F (671°C)	84°F (29°C)
Rubidium (Rb)	1270°F (688°C)	102°F (39°C)

Figure 2.2   Salt is removed from salt mines and refined to make products such as table salt.

Sodium also plays an important role in laboratory work. An electric current passed through a sodium vapor causes the vapor to emit a very precise yellow light when held to a flame. With this light, scientists can calibrate and fine-tune light-measuring devices. This characteristic also makes sodium ideal for use in some highway lights. With the addition of a little electricity, the intense beam emitted by sodium lights remains visible even in foggy conditions. The sensitivity of the human eye to the color yellow means that sodium lamps can improve visibility on the highway, particularly in construction zones.

In addition to its industrial uses, sodium is a common element in our food. Seafood like tuna and sardines is high in sodium, as are foods like liver, butter, cheese, and pickles. Vegetables, typically, are

low in sodium, with the exception of celery and peas. On average, a person needs about 3 grams of sodium a day, but the actual amount of salt consumed on a daily basis varies greatly by culture and diet. In Western cultures, the average sodium intake per person is about 9 grams daily. In comparison, a Japanese diet can contain double this amount of salt. Health experts warn that too much sodium can cause health problems such as high blood pressure.

LITHIUM

Lithium is the lightest of the alkali metals. Like sodium and potassium, it is very reactive and not found in a pure state in nature, but instead is found in compounds. Soft enough to cut with a sharp knife, lithium is especially reactive with water, producing hydrogen gas and lithium hydroxide (LiOH).

Lithium was discovered in 1817 in Stockholm by Swedish chemist Johan August Arfvedson (1792–1841), Arfvedson named the element after the Greek word *lithos,* which means "stone." However, he found lithium challenging to isolate, even by electrolysis. It was not isolated until a few years later, in 1821, by William T. Brande (1788–1866). While Brande succeeded using electrolysis, he was still only able to isolate a tiny amount. Finally, in 1855, the British chemist Augustus Matthiessen (1831–1870) and German chemist Robert Bunsen (1811–1899) worked independently of each other to apply electrolysis to lithium chloride (LiCl), isolating enough lithium to enable the study of its physical and chemical properties. (Bunsen is also responsible for isolating other elements.)

But lithium's history goes back much further. In fact, it was one of three elements, along with hydrogen and helium, that were created in the immediate aftermath of the Big Bang billions of years ago. But lithium does not remain in space for long. Lithium is destroyed in stars where the temperature exceeds several million degrees, which is the temperature found in most of them. However, lithium has proved useful to astronomers for distinguishing

Figure 2.3 Lithium chloride can be extracted from the mineral spodumene ($LiAlSi_2O_6$). Lithium can then be isolated from lithium chloride.

between red dwarf and brown dwarf stars. Both of these kinds of stars are smaller than the Sun, but red dwarf stars are too hot to contain lithium. Brown dwarfs, however, are not. When astronomers measure light patterns of these stars, they can tell which ones are brown dwarfs by their wavelength measurements. A wavelength of 670.7 nanometers indicates the presence of lithium, which means that that star is cooler than a red dwarf.

One primary source for lithium is the mineral spodumene ($LiAlSi_2O_6$) from which lithium chloride can be extracted. Once that occurs, as was first demonstrated by Bunsen and Matthiessen, applying electrolysis to the lithium chloride isolates the lithium.

Among lithium's primary everyday uses is in batteries for watches, calculators, cameras, and other products that need light and compact power sources. Because lithium is a low-density metal, it also has some additional important commercial uses. It makes a great alloy, because it improves the other metal's strength while also making the alloy lighter. For example, lithium mixes with aluminum to form a strong, lightweight alloy that is useful for building bicycle frames, high-speed trains, and even airplanes and spacecraft.

Lithium compounds have several other uses. Lithium oxide is used to make glass and ceramic products. Another compound,

lithium carbonate, is used to produce special types of glass that are resistant to sudden changes in temperature. It is also used in the production of televisions. Some other lithium compounds have also been found to be effective in the treatment of patients with the severe mental illness known as *bipolar disorder*. Patients with this disorder suffer extreme mood swings. How lithium works in the brain's chemical reactions is uncertain, but scientists believe that the element affects how certain brain cells respond to hormones and biological molecules called **neurotransmitters**. Neurotransmitters work in the body's nerve networks to transmit messages related to mood and behaviors.

RUBIDIUM

Rubidium is a very reactive metal that burns spontaneously when exposed to air. When rubidium comes into contact with water, large quantities of hydrogen gas are released, and flames erupt due to extreme heat generated from the reaction.

This metal was first discovered in 1861 by German scientists Robert Bunsen and Gustav Robert Kirchhoff (1824–1887) while they were experimenting with other alkali metals. They named it rubidium after the ruby red lines it emitted when it was heated.

Like other alkali metals, pure rubidium does not exist in nature due to its high reactivity. Rubidium is often found with potassium in soils and minerals such as lepidolite and carnalite. There is little demand for rubidium in industries other than the pharmaceutical industry. The little that is produced—as a byproduct when lithium is extracted from lepidolite—is typically used for research purposes. The compound rubidium chloride has, however, been found effective in treating people with depression.

CESIUM

Cesium is a soft and shiny metal with an extremely low melting point of 84°F (29°C). Its melting point is so low it even melts in

a human hand. (Mercury is the only metal with a lower melting point.) Cesium is not found in its pure form in nature. It is usually found in rocks or soil combined with other elements. Cesium is one of the most reactive of all the alkali metals. It reacts violently with water to release hydrogen gas and cesium hydroxide (CsOH), and reacts with oxygen to produce cesium superoxide (CsO_2). When cesium superoxide comes into contact with water or carbon dioxide, it releases oxygen. Because of this, cesium superoxide is often used to produce breathing equipment used by emergency workers, divers, and firefighters, especially in environments where toxic fumes might be present.

Early research on this metal was done by Carl Plattner (1800–1858) in 1846. Plattner had originally been studying the mineral pollucite, but was puzzled by the fact that he could only account for about 90% of its elements (among them potassium and sodium). Finally, in 1860, the famous chemists Bunsen and Kirchhoff discovered the mysterious metal that made up pollucite's unidentified 10%. When they isolated it, they held it to a Bunsen burner flame, where it gave off a bright blue light. The chemists named this element cesium after the Latin word *coesius,* which means "sky blue."

Cesium plays a big role in making the glass used for manufacturing eyeglasses. This type of glass is submerged in a mixture of molten cesium and sodium. When these two metals are chemically combined, the cesium ions exchange with the sodium ions. The result makes the glass stronger and more resistant to scratching and breaking. Cesium is also used in commercial industries as a catalyst to boost the rate at which other metals react.

The only naturally occurring isotope of cesium is cesium-133, which was chosen by the International Committee of Weights and Measures in 1960 to be the world's official timekeeper. Under this system, one second is equal to the length of time that it takes for 9,192,631,770 vibrations of radiation to be emitted by the cesium-133 atom.

SALT: A LONG HISTORY

Even though sodium was not identified until the early 1800s, historians have determined that many sodium compounds—especially salt—have been in use for thousands of years. Historians have identified Egyptian drawings dating back to 1450 B.C. that depict people working with salt.

Salt has also been an important economic force. In early Roman times, salt was used as a flavoring ingredient. In ancient Greece, slaves were often traded for salt, a practice that prompted the expression "not worth his salt." In fact, the word "salary" comes from the phrase "salarium argentums," which means "salt money" in Latin, referring to the salt allowance often given to Roman soldiers as partial payment for their military service. Salt was also an important commodity carried by early seafaring explorers, who used it in trade with the native people of the lands they visited.

Salt also played a key role in many political and military conflicts, including the Revolutionary War. Taxes on salt in England and the American colonies traditionally supported British monarchs, angering American revolutionaries such as Thomas Paine. During the Revolutionary War, British military leader Lord Howe delivered a severe blow to General George Washington's army when he captured its salt supply.

FRANCIUM

The last element in Group 1, francium, is the heaviest of the alkali metals. It is also one of the most unstable elements, and is produced by the radioactive decay of two other elements, uranium and thorium. Although there are 30 known isotopes of this metal, only one of them, francium-223, exists in nature. The remaining isotopes are produced in nuclear reactors and are too unstable to be studied at

great length. Because of its short half-life, francium is estimated to make up less than 1 ounce of the Earth's crust.

Francium was discovered by Marguerite Perey (1909–1975) in 1939 at the Curie Institute in Paris. She named the metal for France, the country where it was discovered.

SUMMARY

The alkali metals are located in Group 1 of the periodic table. They have low melting points and are the most reactive of the metals. Just as their atomic numbers increase the further down they appear in the group, the intensity of some of their other properties increases, such as reactivity. Their high reactivity also explains why these metals do not exist in pure forms in nature, which made the discovery of them by scientists quite challenging. Today, these metals play significant roles in products and industrial processes.

Alkaline Earth Metals

To the right of the alkali metals is Group 2, the alkaline earth metals. Group 2 has many things in common with Group 1, which is not surprising since they are listed side by side in the periodic table. Both groups are highly reactive and combine easily with other elements, so they are not found free in nature. The alkaline earth metals, like the alkali metals and most other metals, are shiny, malleable, and ductile.

The alkaline earth metals have two valence electrons in their outermost shells. When one of these metals combines with a nonmetal, the alkaline earth metal loses both of its valence electrons and becomes a doubly positively charged ion. One example of this is the compound calcium fluoride (CaF_2). When calcium combines with fluoride, it loses both of its valence electrons to the two fluorine atoms, thus becoming a doubly charged positive ion (Ca^{2+}). This chapter provides a brief discussion of all of the

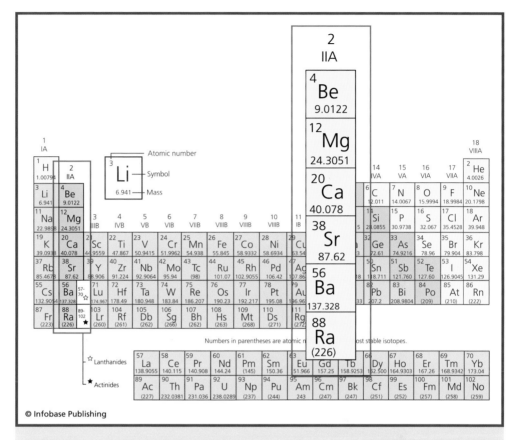

Figure 3.1   Group 2 of the periodic table comprises the alkaline earth metals: beryllium, magnesium, calcium, strontium, barium, and radium.

alkaline earth metals: beryllium, magnesium, calcium, strontium, barium, and radium.

BERYLLIUM

Beryllium is the first element in the alkaline earth metals group, sitting to the right of the alkali metal lithium. In its pure form, this metal is rather hard and has a gray-white appearance. Of all of the metals, beryllium has the lowest density. It is also relatively rare. Although compounds and minerals containing beryllium are found

in the Earth's crust, it ranks number 32 in abundance among the elements. Beryllium is very reactive with oxygen and other elements.

Beryllium was discovered in 1798 by a chemist from France named Louis-Nicolas Vauquelin (1763–1829). Vauquelin was researching the mineral beryl. He discovered that beryl is the principal source of beryllium. Emeralds, along with the blue gem aquamarine, are crystals formed from beryl.

As a pure metal, beryllium has few industrial uses. However, beryllium is transparent to X-rays, and is therefore used in the manufacture of windows for X-ray machines.

Although it may not be valuable as a pure metal, beryllium is often mixed with other metals to form alloys that have industrial uses. One example is beryllium copper alloy, or beryllium bronze. This alloy is not only hard, but does not give off sparks when it is struck. This property makes it a useful material for electrical instruments and hammers that are used in explosive environments, such as in chemical laboratories that use hydrogen or factories that make rocket fuel.

Beryllium is a toxic element, even when present in compounds or alloys. For example, beryllium oxide is a finely powdered compound that, when inhaled, can lead to a painful and deadly disease called *berylliosis*.

MAGNESIUM

Magnesium, the second alkaline earth metal in Group 2, has a silver-white appearance and is lightweight and malleable. Magnesium is chemically reactive, but not extremely reactive like the alkali metals. This metal's name is derived from the mineral magnesite ($MgCO_3$). Magnesium is the seventh most abundant metal in the Earth's crust, and the oceans contain an almost unlimited supply of this metal. One of the most important methods of producing this metal involves extracting magnesium from seawater.

Because magnesium is very light and very strong, it is often used to form alloys that are used to produce structural materials. Magnesium is lighter than iron and aluminum. When magnesium

combines with these metals to form alloys, iron and aluminum are made lighter and stronger. Some examples of these products include aluminum-magnesium alloy ladders, and parts for aircraft. Carmakers also use magnesium because it can make cars weigh less and last longer. Lighter cars are friendlier to the environment because they use less fuel.

In the human body, magnesium ensures that the body's **enzymes** function correctly. Magnesium is also important to green plants. **Chlorophyll**, which is essential in **photosynthesis** (which, in turn, is essential for the survival of green plants), contains magnesium.

Some magnesium compounds are important over-the-counter medicines. For example, milk of magnesia is a suspension of magnesium hydroxide ($Mg[OH]_2$) in water. This creamy liquid suspension is used as an antacid to neutralize excess acid in the stomach. Another magnesium compound remedy is Epsom salts, which are used to treat certain skin rashes. Discovered in Epsom, England, in 1618, these are crystals of magnesium sulfate evaporated from water.

Although seawater is an important source of magnesium, this metal's presence in water that is supplied to homes can be problematic. High concentrations of dissolved magnesium can make water "hard." This hard water interferes with the cleaning power of soaps and detergents, forming soap scum. The magnesium is removed from the water through a process called *softening*. This process replaces magnesium with sodium, which does not interfere as much with detergents and soaps.

CALCIUM

Calcium is the fifth most abundant element in the Earth's crust and is also found in living organisms. In humans and other mammals, teeth and bones contain calcium. The shells of marine organisms are made of a compound called *calcium carbonate* ($CaCO_3$). When these organisms die, these shells form coral reefs like those found in the Florida Keys and the Bahamas. Sir Humphrey Davy first isolated and identified calcium in 1808.

Calcium is fairly reactive—too reactive to be found as a pure metal in nature. When it reacts with water, it forms calcium hydroxide [$Ca(OH)_2$], and when it reacts with oxygen, it forms calcium oxide (CaO), or lime, one of calcium's most common compounds. (Limestone is a rock primarily made out of calcium carbonate.) Calcium compounds are used to make building materials such as concrete, marble, and gypsum.

Like magnesium, calcium can also be found in large concentrations dissolved in water supplies and can interfere with the cleaning powers of soaps and detergents. When the calcium atom loses two electrons and becomes positively charged (Ca^{2+}), it becomes able to form ionic bonds with negatively charged ions. When dissolved in water, these calcium ions are known as *hardness ions* because they help form hard water. More problems, especially with plumbing, can occur if this hard water also contains bicarbonate ions (HCO_3^-). When water containing this compound is heated, the bicarbonate ions transform into carbon dioxide gas (CO_2) and carbonate ions (CO_3^-). The heat forces the gaseous carbon dioxide out of the water. The remaining carbonate and calcium ions react to form calcium carbonate ($CaCO_3$) that takes the form of an insoluble substance, which sticks to hot water pipes and boiler walls. The buildup of this substance along the wall slows the flow of water through the pipes.

STRONTIUM

Strontium is a silvery and soft metal that is very reactive. When it is finely divided into a powder, it burns spontaneously in air. Its primary sources are two minerals, celestite and strontianite. In 1789, the Irish scientist Adair Crawford (1748–1795) first identified the element (along with the mineral strontianite) and named the element for Strontian, the village in Scotland where he made the discovery. (Crawford was actually studying the chemical reaction between a mineral called *witherite* ($BaCO_3$) and hydrochloric acid (HCl) at the time, but was frustrated when he failed to get the

Figure 3.2 Strontium can be extracted from the mineral celestite ($SrSO_4$).

results he expected.) In 1808, the famous chemist Sir Humphrey Davy was the first to isolate the metal through the electrolysis of strontium chloride ($SrCl_2$) and mercuric oxide (HgO).

Because strontium carbonate gives off a red color when it burns, this compound is often used in fireworks and for flares, such as those used to alert drivers on roads and highways. Beyond this application, strontium does not have many commercial or industrial uses.

BARIUM

Like other alkaline earth metals, barium is a soft, silvery white metal. Discovered by Humphrey Davy in 1808, its primary sources are witherite, which is a type of barium carbonate ($BaCO_3$), and baryte, a type of barium sulfate ($BaSO_4$).

Barium burns quickly in the air and reacts with water to produce hydrogen. Some barium compounds can be quite toxic. For instance, ingesting the soluble form of barium chloride can damage the heart, causing an erratic heartbeat—a condition known as ventricular fibrillation. However, if barium is in an insoluble form, it is not toxic, and in fact has some valuable applications. For example, barium sulfate can help doctors see a patient's organs

CHEMISTRY'S MOST FAMOUS COUPLE: MARIE AND PIERRE CURIE

When Marie Sklodowska was growing up in Poland in the late 1800s, there were not any real education opportunities for her after she completed high school. After saving some money, she went to Paris in 1891, where her older sister was studying medicine. Marie began studying at the Sorbonne, and soon met the French chemist Pierre Curie in 1894. They were married a year later, forming one of the most famous science research teams in history.

The Curies focused their early research on studying radioactivity and the energy produced as radioactive atoms decayed. They discovered polonium and radium, and identified thorium as a radioactive element. Marie and Pierre's lives were characterized by poverty, even though they were celebrated in the world of science. Marie and Pierre shared a Nobel Prize in physics. Marie won another Nobel in chemistry. Unfortunately, Pierre was killed when he was run down by a horse-drawn carriage in 1906, so he was unable to share the second Nobel Prize with his wife. Marie died in 1934 of leukemia, which she likely developed after working throughout her life with high levels of radiation. The following year, the Curies' eldest daughter Iréne received a Nobel Prize in Chemistry with her husband Frédéric Joliot, for their work with radioactive elements.

Figure 3.3   Marie Curie won two Nobel Prizes for her work with radioactive elements.

in an X-ray image. Barium sulfate is a dense salt that is thick and opaque in X-ray images. If a patient ingests this compound, it temporarily spreads throughout the digestive tract. The barium sulfate absorbs the X-rays, allowing the intestines and organs to appear white against a black background in the X-ray picture.

Because barium reacts so quickly with oxygen and moisture, it has few commercial or industrial uses. But because it is a silvery white substance and has low solubility in water, it is often used as a whitener in photos, writing paper, and plastics.

RADIUM

Radium, the last metal in the alkaline earth metal group, has an intense white color and is extremely radioactive. In the dark, it glows and gives off a soft blue color. The French husband and wife chemist team Marie (1867–1934) and Pierre Curie (1859–1906) discovered radium in 1898. Along with the discovery of the electron and Albert Einstein's theory of relativity, the discovery of radium marked the beginning of the modern era of science.

Before radium's dangerous radioactive properties were understood, it was used to make paints for watches and clocks that could be seen in the dark. Currently, radium is used in medical facilities like hospitals and other treatment centers to produce a radioactive gas called *radon*, which is used to treat cancer patients.

SUMMARY

Group 2 of the periodic table contains the alkaline earth metals: beryllium, magnesium, calcium, strontium, barium, and radium. These elements are similar to the alkali metals in that they are shiny, ductile, and malleable. The alkaline earth metals have two electrons in their outermost shell. Although they are not as reactive as the alkali metals, the alkaline earth metals are rarely found pure in nature.

Transition Metals

The transition metals are located in Groups 3 through 12 in the periodic table. They are in this category because they are the elements in transition between Groups 1 and 2 and Groups 13 through 18. Groups 1 and 2 are considered the first block in the periodic table, and the transition elements are called the second block. Unlike the less stable metals in the first block, many of these elements are often found pure in nature. In addition, when the transition metals combine with other elements, the resulting compounds are often brightly colored. For example, colorful paints in shades like cadmium yellow and cobalt blue are made from compounds that contain transition elements.

This chapter examines some of these transition elements: iron, cobalt, nickel, copper, silver, gold, zinc, cadmium, and mercury. The first three elements—iron, cobalt, and nickel—are often called the

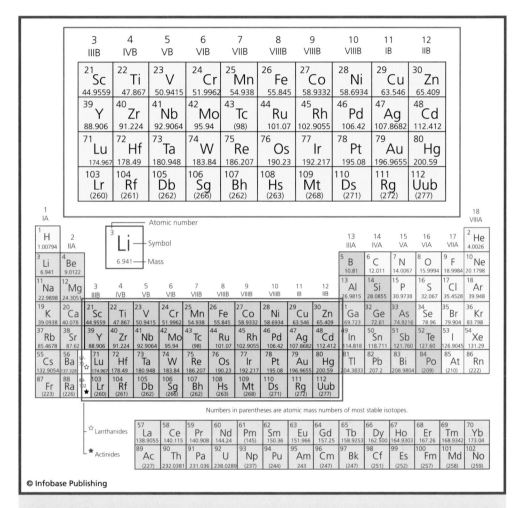

Figure 4.1   The transition metals are found in Groups 3 through 12 of the periodic table.

iron triad. All three of the elements are used to make metal alloys such as steel. Copper, silver, and gold are called the coinage metals, because they are often used in coin-making. In addition, this chapter looks at the lanthanides and the actinides. While these are part of the transitional metals, they are often extracted and displayed alongside the main portion of the periodic table.

Figure 4.2　Iron is known for its strength and is commonly used to build large constructions, such as bridges.

IRON

One of the most common metals in the world, iron is used in the manufacture of products we encounter every day. Iron is used to build bridges and buildings, as well as machines, tools, and automobiles. This metal is also important to our health. In the blood, it carries oxygen throughout the body to places where it is needed.

Iron has played a significant role in the development of civilization. Beginning around 1100 B.C., during what was known as the Iron Age, people learned how to extract and refine iron from the rocks they dug from the earth. Once people learned to mine this metal, they were able to fashion it into tools and weapons to defend themselves, hunt for food, and build shelter. These iron materials proved more durable than those produced during the previous Bronze Age (3000 B.C.).

Iron is the fourth most abundant element in the Earth's crust. Iron is often found in the minerals hematite, magnetite, and marcasite. Large deposits of iron-bearing minerals are found primarily in Australia, Canada, France, India, South Africa, and the United States. The iron used in industry comes from these mineral deposits. In addition, the interior of Earth—called the *core*—is believed to be composed primarily of iron. Earth's interior is extremely hot—hot enough to melt iron into a molten state.

Pure forms of this metal are rarely found in nature because it combines easily with water and air to form **rust**, a hydrated oxide of iron. Rust's reddish material does not stick to the iron's surface for long. It crumbles off, continuously exposing new layers of fresh iron to the air. This weakens the iron, causing it to eventually disintegrate.

One of iron's well-known properties is its **magnetism**, which is due to the arrangement of the atoms. In iron, groups of atoms, called *domains*, align so that they point in one direction, causing *magnetic* **dipoles** to form. (Materials that are not magnetic have domains but their domains do not point in the same direction.) Three metals—iron, cobalt, and nickel—are strong magnets. Of these three, iron is the strongest magnet because its atoms are

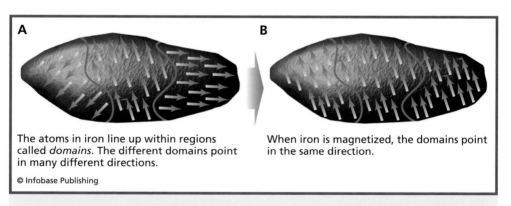

A

The atoms in iron line up within regions called *domains*. The different domains point in many different directions.

© Infobase Publishing

B

When iron is magnetized, the domains point in the same direction.

Figure 4.3   An illustration of iron's magnetism; iron is a powerful magnet because of the properties of its atoms.

spaced the ideal distance apart for the dipoles to strongly affect each other. When iron is in its natural state, the domains are pointed in different directions and cancel each other out. However, when iron is placed in a magnetic field, the domains all point in the same direction and become magnetized. When the iron is taken away from the magnetic source, the iron then returns to its natural state.

The iron churning in the Earth's core also turns our planet into a giant magnet. Magnetic fields surround Earth, coming together at two magnetic points: the magnetic north and south poles. These two points are located near the geographic North and South Poles.

COBALT

Cobalt is extracted from an ore called *cobaltite*, which is a compound of cobalt, arsenic, and sulfur. This element is often used in compounds and alloys that are added to steel to increase its strength. In addition, cobalt is often mixed with tungsten and copper to form an alloy known as stellite, which is a popular product because it retains its durability and hardness even at high temperatures.

Like iron, cobalt also has magnetic properties. Cobalt's magnetic powers are not as strong as those of iron, but, compared to iron, cobalt is able to retain its magnetism at higher temperatures. Cobalt is used in the production of a substance called *alnico*—an

TABLE 4.1: THE MOST ABUNDANT METALS IN THE EARTH'S CRUST	
METAL (CHEMICAL SYMBOL)	PARTS PER MILLION
Iron (Fe)	41,000
Calcium (Ca)	41,000
Sodium (Na)	23,000
Potassium (K)	21,000
Magnesium (Mg)	21,000

alloy of aluminum, nickel, and cobalt. Alnico has powerful magnetic properties and is used to make industrial magnets. Like cobalt, magnets made of alnico retain their magnetism at high temperatures.

Cobalt has many commercial uses, in addition to making magnets. Because of its bluish color, artists and manufacturers use it to make pottery, stained glass, tiles, and certain kinds of jewelry. In the nineteenth century, glassmakers used cobalt to make bottles.

This transition metal also has nutritional importance. Small amounts of cobalt are present in meat and dairy products as a part of vitamin B12. Cobalt is needed to help make red blood cells. Only small amounts of cobalt are needed in a healthy diet.

NICKEL

A silver metal, nickel is rarely found in its pure form on the Earth's surface, although scientists believe that there is a significant amount present—along with iron—in the planet's core. Nickel deposits are often found in meteorites that were formed about the same time as Earth. Nickel is primarily mined from sulfur ores.

Pure nickel was first isolated in 1751. Like cobalt, nickel was used to color glass, though nickel compounds turn glass and other substances green rather than blue. Because nickel is resistant to corrosion, it is often combined with other metals to form alloys that resist oxidation. A process known as electroplating uses nickel to coat the surface of metals that are vulnerable to corrosion, like iron or steel. Stainless steel is an example of a product made from nickel: almost half the nickel that is mined each year is used to manufacture it. Also composed of chromium, stainless steel is extremely resistant to corrosion. Another nickel alloy is monel, which is made with copper. Monel is hard and resistant to corrosion, making it ideal for commercial marine applications such as the manufacture of boat propellers. The heating parts in toasters and electric ovens are made from an alloy called *nichrome*, which is another metal, made from chromium and nickel.

Of course, one of the most common uses for nickel is coin-making, specifically, the five-cent coin. The nickel coin is an alloy made of copper and nickel. Another important and common use for this metal is the nickel-cadmium battery, which contains a nickel-oxide electrode. This battery is rechargeable, making it ideal for calculators, computers, and other small electrical appliances.

Nickel can pose some minor health hazards to people who come into contact with it. For example, both nickel in solution and the nickel in stainless steel are known to cause a skin irritation known as nickel itch, which is a form of dermatitis. Stainless steel watches, jewelry, and glasses frames have all been known to cause this irritation. More serious health hazards can come from inhaling nickel dust. In nickel mining and other industrial environments where nickel is used, inhaling the dust has been linked to nasal and lung cancer.

COPPER

Copper is one of the most well-known metals, and it is used in many areas in everyday life. For instance, the pipes that carry water and waste throughout homes and other constructions are made of copper. Copper's ductile properties allow it to be drawn into wires. In addition, as an excellent conductor of electricity, copper wire is used in homes, offices, and other buildings to transmit electrical energy from wall outlets to electrical appliances.

The name *copper* comes from the Latin word *cuprum,* which means "from Cyprus." Cyprus is an island located in the Mediterranean Sea, south of Turkey. Ancient Romans mined copper from this island. Other ancient societies mined copper from ores. At that time, it was easy to refine the copper and make it into jewelry. But because it was a soft metal, unlike iron, it was not used in the production of weapons or tools.

At one time, copper was commonly used in making pennies. However, production of pennies using copper stopped in 1981. The penny is now treated with a copper coating to give the coin its reddish brown-color. Copper was also formerly used to make buttons

Figure 4.4 Copper is easy to extract from nature, and it is a good conductor of electricity. Plus, it can be easily drawn into wires.

for police uniforms. Manufacturers like to use copper because it does not react easily with air and water. However, this metal is not entirely resistant to corrosion. Over time, copper corrodes in the atmosphere and forms a green layer of either copper carbonate ($CuCO_3$) or copper sulfate ($CuSO_4$). These coatings, also known as patinas, provide a weatherproof layer to statues and protect the copper from further corrosion. For example, patina covers New York's Statue of Liberty. Originally created in France and made of copper plates, the statue was restored in honor of its centennial in 1986. While the restorers worked hard to preserve the patina, the interior of the copper skin needed to be cleaned. Many older monuments all over the world are also made of copper. Many people consider the green patina that eventually develops on the structures to be quite beautiful.

SILVER

Unlike most metals, silver is found in nature in its natural, free state. It is also mined from ores such as argentite. A soft metal, silver is both ductile and malleable. This metal is considered the best conductor of heat and electricity of all the metals. Silver can be rare to find, which explains why it is expensive to buy objects made of

silver. Because it is rather expensive, silver is not typically used to make electrical wiring, although it is used in the manufacture of high-quality electronic appliances.

Like copper, silver was used in many ancient civilizations. Its symbol, Ag, comes from the word *argentum*, which is the Latin

LADY LIBERTY: STILL STANDING TALL

Copper weight: 62,000 lbs (28,122 kilograms)
Steel weight: 250,000 lbs (113,400 kg)
Thickness of copper sheeting covering the statue: 0.1 inch (2.37 millimeters), approximately the thickness of two pennies.

In April 1886, France gave the United States the Statue of Liberty in recognition of the friendship between the two countries that was established during the American Revolution. One hundred years later, however, certain areas of the statue—particularly the torch, the hand supporting the torch, and the crown—needed to be repaired and restored. Although the copper skin was in good shape, the interior of the copper shell

Figure 4.5   The Statue of Liberty has a copper skin that has oxidized to a greenish color.

had layers of coal tar, aluminum, and lead that needed to be cleaned off. The restoration project was completed in 1986, in time for the statue's centennial celebration.

word for silver. Historians believe that the great ancient civilizations around Athens, Greece, relied heavily on local silver deposits. These mines are believed to have operated throughout the Roman Empire. There were also large silver deposits in Germany. Throughout the Middle Ages, silver mines in Germany supplied most of Europe with this metal. Today, only about 25% of silver is obtained from silver mines. Most silver is produced as a by-product of the refining of other metals, such as zinc, gold, and copper. Mexico, Peru, the United States, and Australia continue to produce the most silver.

One of silver's most common uses is for making jewelry. Typically, copper is alloyed with silver to increase the hardness. For example, sterling silver jewelry is composed of 7.5% copper, with silver rings and bracelets containing as much as 20% copper. The amount of silver in jewelry is described in terms of its "fineness" and is expressed as 10 times the percentage of silver in the particular piece. Because sterling silver is 93% silver, it has a fineness of 930. Many pieces of silverware have a fineness of 800 because they are composed of 80% silver. For thousands of years, silver was also used to make coins, but it was not durable enough. In the United States, silver coins are no longer in use: their silvery appearance is due to a copper-nickel alloy that is used in their manufacture.

Silver is also used as a coating because of the shiny luster it gives off when it is polished. **Electroplating** gives a silver coating to jewelry and eating utensils that are made of less expensive metals. Electroplating involves connecting an electrically positive terminal, or **anode**, from a power source, such as a battery, to a bar of silver. The negative terminal, or **cathode**, is then connected to the object to be plated. While the electrical current enters the power source through the anode, the current leaves through the cathode. The object is then placed in a bath of a silver cyanide mixture, and as the current flows through the battery, a silvery coating spreads over the object.

While silver is not very reactive, it does eventually **tarnish** in the form of a black film. This film is actually the compound silver

sulfide. Another sulfide compound, hydrogen sulfide, which comes from the air, decays vegetables and other kinds of food It also reacts with silver to tarnish it, so if silver comes in contact with sulfur-containing foods like eggs or mustard, it can tarnish over a short period of time.

GOLD

Gold is well known for its monetary value—gold coins and bars have been used as currency for thousands of years. It is traded on international financial markets, and the health of a nation's economy is measured against the changing prices of gold.

In addition to its currency value, gold is considered the most precious metal because of its beautiful brilliant yellow color, its durability, and its resistance to corrosion. Gold's chemical symbol—Au—comes from the Latin word *aurum*, which translates to "shining dawn." The durability and resistance of this metal is due to the fact that gold is very unreactive. Compounds such as nitric acid have little impact on this metal, although it does dissolve slowly in solutions of hydrochloric and nitric acids.

Because of gold's resistance to corrosion, it is often found in its pure state in nature, most often as nuggets or flakes, although it can also be found as deposits of a type of mineral called a *telluride*. Gold can be found all over the world—typically near deposits of quartz and pyrite. In the United States, most of the gold comes from Nevada and South Dakota. Outside of the United States, most of the gold comes from South Africa. Sometimes gold can be found in seawater, although the quantity is too small to make for profitable mining.

Gold is also the most ductile and malleable of all the metals. Gold is often pounded into thin leaves for decoration. One ounce of gold can be pounded flat to cover an area of 300 square feet (91.44 square meters). This ductility and resistance to corrosion—as well as its ability to reflect infrared radiation—make gold an excellent coating for space vehicles. Gold coatings are also used in dentistry

and in the production of electronics. When used as fillings or replacements, gold teeth can last for many decades. In electronics, switches and connectors are often coated with gold. Because gold resists corrosion, coating these switches with gold helps them to maintain their efficiency and conductivity over time.

Despite its durability, gold is actually a very soft metal. When used in the creation of jewelry, gold is often alloyed with another metal, such as nickel or copper, to increase its hardness. Gold's purity is expressed in a measurement called carats. Pure gold is known as 24-carat, whereas most jewelry is 18 carats. The percentage of gold in a piece of jewelry can be determined by dividing the carat measurement by 24, then multiplying by 100. For example, an 18-carat gold ring is 75% gold (18 divided by 24, then multiplied by 100). In 18-carat jewelry, gold is often alloyed with copper and silver. While gold is yellow, copper is red, so adding the copper to gold increases the redness of the jewelry. Adding silver makes the gold paler.

PANNING FOR GOLD: THE FORTY-NINERS

When gold was discovered in California in 1849, thousands of people from across the country and abroad descended on the territory, hoping to strike it rich. Many of them used a technique called panning, in which the miners—or "forty-niners," as they were called—took gold-flecked sand and swirled it around shallow pans. The density of gold is about nine times greater than that of sand or gravel. Therefore, as the miners swirled the sand around their pans, the sand and gravel would wash over the rim, leaving behind the much denser gold in the pan.

ZINC

Although zinc is not an abundant element compared to metals such as copper and silver, trace amounts are found in Earth's crust. Because it is rather reactive, it is rarely found pure in nature. Its mineral sources are compounds that contain zinc sulfides, also known as sphalerite or zincblende. It is a reactive element, but it quickly forms a hard oxide coating when it is in its purest form. This coating prevents further reaction with air, therefore protecting the metal from corrosion. Approximately 90% of the zinc produced in the United States is used to form galvanized steel. Galvanization is the process by which steel is covered with a layer of zinc coating to make it corrosion resistant, which prevents air or water from coming into contact with the steel. Galvanizing is done by either dipping the steel object into molten zinc, or through electrolysis, in which zinc is electrically deposited onto the steel product. Chain-link fences, garbage cans, and a number of other household products are made out of galvanized steel.

Another important use for zinc is the dry-cell battery, which is the energy source for everything from electronic toys to household objects such as remote controls. The battery has an outer metal shell that serves as the anode and protects an inner case made of zinc. It also contains a carbon rod that serves as the cathode. Dry-cell batteries typically generate an electric force of about 1.5 volts.

Zinc is also a primary metal in the penny coin, which used to be made of copper. In addition, zinc can be mixed with copper to form brass, which is a very useful alloy because of its durability and hardness. Another useful compound is zinc oxide. Made by burning zinc vapor in air, zinc oxide is used to make white paints. Used as an ointment, zinc oxide makes a good sunscreen because it blocks the Sun's harmful ultraviolet rays that damage the skin. Zinc oxide also has another important property: it is photoconductive, which means that it conducts electricity better when exposed to light. For example, a photocopier contains a photoconductive plate that is sometimes made with zinc oxide. When this plate is electrically

charged and then exposed to a printed document, a light is passed through the document and then onto the plate. The plate has two parts that react to this charge. The portions of the plate that are lighted become more conductive and allow the electrical charge to flow away from the plate. The rest of the plate, the dark parts, are poorly conductive so they remain charged, and correspond to the ink on the document. Toner—a black, positively charged powder—is then spread over the surface of the plate, sticking to the parts of the plate that are still negatively charged. The image from the document is then reproduced and transferred to a new piece of paper through heating.

CADMIUM

A soft, silvery metal, cadmium has chemical properties that are similar to those of zinc. However, compared to zinc, cadmium is very rare. Cadmium sulfide ores are one source of this metal. It is also present in zinc ores, but in such small amounts that it is usually only produced as a by-product of zinc refining. Cadmium's discovery is even linked with zinc. In 1817, the German chemist Friedrich Strohmeyer (1776–1835) discovered cadmium when he was studying the compound zinc oxide.

Like zinc, cadmium is used to electroplate steel to protect it from corrosion. However, because cadmium is rare, it is more expensive and so it is used less often than zinc. This metal can also cause health problems in humans, including high blood pressure and kidney failure. Small amounts of cadmium are present in tobacco leaves, exposing cigarette smokers to dangerous levels of this metal. Another disadvantage is that waste from electroplating industries that use cadmium has polluted lakes and other water sources.

One of cadmium's primary uses is in the manufacture of batteries. Nickel-cadmium batteries, also known as nicad batteries, can be recharged many times with only small losses of efficiency. This makes nicad batteries more durable and longer lasting than rechargeable lead batteries. Nicad batteries are also more convenient

because, like common dry-cell batteries, they are portable. Another important use for cadmium is in nuclear reactors because of its ability to absorb neutrons and stop nuclear reactions. Cadmium is also part of an important alloy called *Wood's metal*, which is made up of bismuth and about 12.5% cadmium. This alloy has a very low melting point for a metal—158°F (70°C)—which makes it an excellent sealer for the overhead sprinklers that are used for fire protection in many homes and buildings. When the sprinkler seal heats up from a fire, the seal breaks and releases the water to douse the fire.

MERCURY

Mercury is a unique element. An extremely heavy metal, it is the only metallic element that exists in liquid form at room temperature. This silvery white metal is a good conductor of electricity, but it is a poor conductor of heat, which is unusual for metals. Scientists have shown that mercury has been known to humanity for thousands of years. People in ancient China knew of the metal, and samples of it have been found in Egyptian tombs dating back to 1500 B.C. While its name comes from the planet Mercury, its chemical symbol, Hg, comes from the Latin word *hydragyrum*, which means "liquid silver." Mercury's primary ore is cinnabar, which is also known as vermillion. This ore, found chiefly in Spain and Italy, contains an abundance of mercury sulfide compounds. Mercury is extracted from cinnabar by heating the ore and then condensing the resulting vapor.

With a melting point of about –38°F (–39°C) and a boiling point of about 674°F (–357°C), mercury remains in a liquid form over a wide range of temperatures, which makes it useful for many home and laboratory products. Some thermometers, thermostats that regulate cooling and heating systems in the home, wall switches, and fluorescent light bulbs all contain mercury. Another interesting characteristic of mercury is its high surface tension. For example, when a thermometer that contains mercury breaks, the

Figure 4.6 This is a sample of the ore cinnabar (vermillion). Cinnabar contains high concentrations of mercury sulfide and is the chief ore from which mercury is extracted.

mercury spills out and forms small spheres that roll around without sticking to any surface. This makes mercury hard to collect.

Mercury is also able to dissolve other metals, such as gold, to form alloys known as **amalgams**. For example, mercury is often used to extract gold from its ore. The gold is dissolved in mercury to form an amalgam, which is then heated until the mercury vaporizes, leaving the gold behind.

Although this heavy metal has many practical uses, mercury is an extremely toxic element to humans because it can be absorbed into the body through the skin and the lungs. If absorbed, mercury reacts with enzymes and disrupts the body's ability to carry out vital functions. People who suffer prolonged exposure to mercury develop serious problems, including loss of memory.

LANTHANIDES AND ACTINIDES

These metals are considered transition metals, but you may notice that they are typically separated from the rest of the periodic table in order for the groups and periods of the table to be displayed in a convenient format. The lanthanides, also known as lanthanoids, are elements with atomic numbers between 57 and 70, and are named

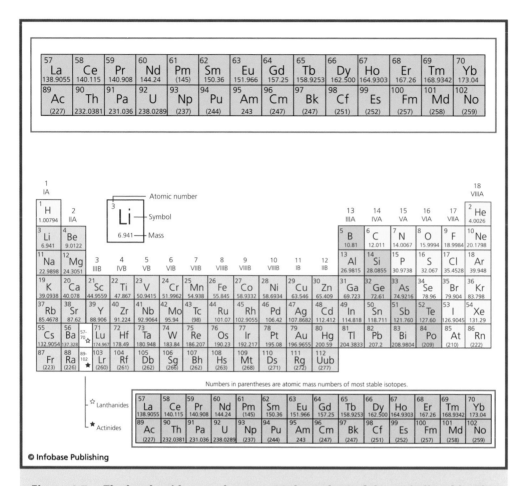

57 La 138.9055	58 Ce 140.115	59 Pr 140.908	60 Nd 144.24	61 Pm (145)	62 Sm 150.36	63 Eu 151.966	64 Gd 157.25	65 Tb 158.9253	66 Dy 162.500	67 Ho 164.9303	68 Er 167.26	69 Tm 168.9342	70 Yb 173.04
89 Ac (227)	90 Th 232.0381	91 Pa 231.036	92 U 238.0289	93 Np (237)	94 Pu (244)	95 Am 243	96 Cm (247)	97 Bk (247)	98 Cf (251)	99 Es (252)	100 Fm (257)	101 Md (258)	102 No (259)

© Infobase Publishing

Figure 4.7   The lanthanides are elements 57 through 70 of the periodic table. The actinides are 89 through 102.

for the first element in the series, lanthanum. For a long time, the lanthanides were known as the rare earth elements. This designation is not entirely accurate, however, because not all of these elements are rare.

For many years, lanthanide elements had little or no commercial use. The one exception was a mixture of lanthanide oxides known as Misch metal, which is used to improve the strength of steel alloys. More recently, scientists have developed new uses for

lanthanide metals. Some of these compounds are used to make color television sets. Alloys of samarium and cobalt have electromagnetic properties. Salts made from europium compounds are

EXAMINING THE TRANSFERIUM ELEMENTS

Some of the elements in the last row of the periodic table are placed in a special category known as the transferium elements. These are elements with an atomic number greater than 101.

The transferium elements have unstable nuclei, and therefore have extremely short half-lives. For some of these elements, the longest-lived isotopes have half-lives of only a few seconds. Because they have such short half-lives, it is difficult to determine their behavior and properties. However, what is known is that these elements play no role in the human body, the environment, or our economy or industry.

TABLE 4.2 HALF-LIVES OF SOME TRANSFERIUM ELEMENTS

TRANSFERIUM ELEMENT NAME (CHEMICAL SYMBOL)	HALF LIFE OF LONGEST OCCURRING ISOTOPE
Mendelevium (Md)	51.5 days
Nobelium (No)	55 seconds
Lawrencium (Lr)	35 seconds
Rutherfordium (Rf)	4–5 seconds
Dubnium (Db)	40 seconds
Seaborgium (Sg)	30 seconds
Bohrium (Bh)	15 seconds

used to make postage stamps. Cerium is used to polish glass and as a coating for the inner walls of self-cleaning ovens.

The actinides, or actinoids, have atomic numbers between 89 and 102 and are named for the first element in that series, actinium. The actinides are often called the *transuranium* elements and include the three heaviest naturally occurring elements in the periodic table—thorium, protactinium, and uranium. Protactinium is rare, but uranium and thorium are found in significant amounts in the Earth's crust. The remaining actinides are synthetic, which means they are produced through artificial means.

Of all the actinides, uranium is probably the most well known. Discovered in 1789, it plays a key part in the manufacture of nuclear weapons and reactors. Its radioactive properties were first identified and understood in the late 1800s.

In addition to uranium, only a few other actinides have commercial uses. Currently, thorium is used to manufacture portable gas lanterns. Thorium oxide is used to make high-quality glass and is also a catalyst in various industrial processes. Plutonium also has commercial uses in uranium reactors and as fuel in nuclear reactors.

SUMMARY

In this chapter, we learned about the transition metals, which are located in Groups 3 through 12 in the periodic table. Compared to other metals, the transition elements are more stable and are therefore more often found pure in nature. The transition metals also include the lanthanides and actinides, two groups that are often displayed separately in the periodic table. The actinides contain the three heaviest naturally occurring elements in the periodic table—thorium, protactinium, and uranium.

Metals and Chemical Reactions

In a **chemical reaction**, atoms are rearranged to form new substances. At the beginning of a chemical reaction, the elements or compounds are called **reactants.** At the end of the reaction, new substances called **products** are produced. There are different kinds of chemical reactions. For example, **synthesis** is when reactants combine to form a new compound, and **analysis** is the breakdown of a reactant into its primary elements.

Materials can be manipulated through physical or chemical means. With physical changes, the material is only temporarily transformed. For example, when water boils, it produces water vapor—which is essentially water in gas form. When the vapor cools, it changes back to liquid. If the water is frozen, it becomes a solid. None of these processes represent permanent changes to the water, but rather temporary changes to its form. Another example is when two solids like sulfur and iron are mixed. This physical

change can be reversed by placing a magnet in the mixture, which will attract the iron and separate it from the sulfur.

Chemical changes occur when the chemical composition of the material is actually altered. For example, if sulfur and iron are heated together, it becomes impossible to separate the individual elements through ordinary means. Thus, the result is a new substance. This new substance would require a chemical reaction to separate out the reactants.

Metals form numerous different compounds. Group 1 metals— the alkali metals—are highly reactive with many different substances, including air and water. The alkali earth metals—Group 2—are slightly less reactive than the Group 1 metals. Metals can also form an alloy, in which two or more metals mix but are not chemically combined. Many metals are catalysts for reactions, which means that the metallic element accelerates a chemical reaction. At the end of the reaction, however, the metal remains unchanged. In this chapter, we look at the different kinds of chemical reactions that involve metallic elements.

ENERGY SHIFT

During a chemical reaction, there is always a change of energy. Typically, this energy takes the form of heat. If heat is given off as a result of a reaction, the reaction is said to be **exothermic**. If heat is absorbed, the reaction is called **endothermic**. Light is another form of energy that can be used to drive a chemical reaction. For example, plants need to produce carbohydrates to keep their trunks, leaves, and roots healthy. The water and carbon dioxide that plants take in from the soil and air react with the light energy from the Sun to produce carbohydrates, which is the process called **photosynthesis**. Reactions can also be caused by electricity. Metals are good conductors of electricity, making electricity a common factor in many reactions that involve metals. In fact, for some of the more highly reactive metals, such as sodium, electricity is necessary to separate them from compounds.

Before we examine the various kinds of reactions, we need to look at how chemical reactions are described in chemical equations. Chemical equations represent a shorthand method of describing reactions, and are based on the principle known as the

EARLY CHEMISTRY AND THE ANCIENT WORLD

After learning to use fire, early peoples began to experiment with not only cooking and pottery, but also began to investigate how fire could be used to extract metals from ore and other materials.

In ancient Greece, people began to think about matter—what it was, where it came from, and what its different forms were. They combined their theories with religious and mystical ideas. One of their beliefs was that base metals like lead and copper could be transformed into gold, which was believed to be the most perfect and precious substance. This practice was known as alchemy, and early chemists who worked on this were called alchemists. In addition to their early work with metals, alchemists developed a technique called distillation, a process of separating liquid chemical mixtures through evaporation and subsequent condensation and cooling. Through distillation, these early chemists were able to prepare oils and perfumes, as well as mineral acids.

Through this work with chemicals and mixtures, these early scientists began to develop medical theories about the human body. They believed that disease and illness were caused by an imbalance in the body's chemical system. To restore this balance and make the body healthy, certain chemicals or medications needed to be added to the body. This theory is one of the foundations of modern medicine.

law of the conservation of mass, which says that the starting mass of the reactants is equal to the mass of the products.

CHEMICAL EQUATIONS

Let's say that in the laboratory, nickel chloride ($NiCl_2$) and sodium hydroxide (NaOH) are dissolved in water, producing a precipitate of solid nickel hydroxide [$Ni(OH)_2$] plus sodium chloride (NaCl) dissolved in water. This description is important because it tells exactly what is going on in the reaction, but a simpler way of expressing this reaction is with a chemical equation, which uses formulas and symbols to describe the same reactions.

The equation for the nickel chloride and sodium hydroxide looks like this:

$$NiCl_2(aq) + 2NaOH(aq) \rightarrow Ni(OH)_2(s) + 2NaCl(aq)$$

The number "2" that precedes sodium hydroxide (NaOH) and sodium chloride (NaCl) are called **coefficients**. Recall that according to the law of the conservation of mass, the same amount of matter present at the beginning of a reaction is present at the

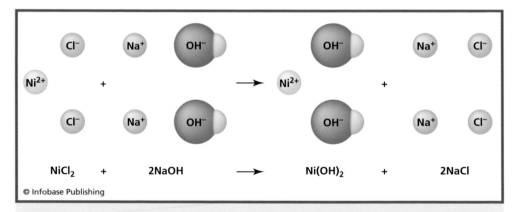

Figure 5.1   The chemical reaction between nickel chloride ($NiCl_2$) and sodium hydroxide (NaOH) produces nickel hydroxide [$Ni(OH)_2$] and sodium chloride (NaCl).

TABLE 5.1: SYMBOLS USED IN CHEMICAL EQUATIONS	
SYMBOL	**MEANING**
→	Produces
+	Plus
(*s*)	Solid
(*l*)	Liquid
(*g*)	Gas
(*aq*)	Substance dissolved in water or aqueous solution
Heat →	Reactants are heated
Light →	Reactants are exposed to light
Electricity →	Electricity is applied to reactants

end of the reaction. This means that during a reaction, the total number of atoms must be conserved, which is reflected in this equation.

The following section takes a closer look at specific reactions that involve metals. These include oxidation, combustion, reactions between mercury and other metals, and reactions between metals and electricity. Interactions between metals and acids and bases will also be examined.

OXIDATION

Many metals are highly reactive with air and water. The metals combine with the oxygen in air and water to create a new substance. This process is called **oxidation**.

One example of oxidation is rusting. Iron—and iron products, including steel—are especially vulnerable to rusting because iron combines so easily with oxygen. When iron combines with oxygen, it forms iron oxide. This is also known as rust—the brittle brown flakes that form on the surface of iron. Rust builds on the iron's surface, corroding the outer layers. As the outer layer is eaten away,

the inner layers are exposed to oxygen and also become rusted. This process ultimately weakens the product.

When many of the most reactive metals—those in Groups 1 and 2—come into contact with water, they release hydrogen and produce a metal hydroxide compound. An example of a Group 1 hydroxide formation is the reaction that takes place when sodium interacts with water. When a piece of sodium is dropped into water, the sodium starts fizzing. Hydrogen gas is produced. The reaction also produces the colorless solid sodium hydroxide, which is dissolved in the water. This reaction is exothermic, meaning it

THE BIRTH OF MODERN CHEMISTRY

By the 1700s, the study of chemistry began moving from alchemy to the science we know today. It was during this time that the famous French chemist Antoine Lavoisier (1743–1794) determined that, the mass of the reactants equals the mass of the products in a chemical reaction. This is known as the conservation of mass principle.

Lavoisier discovered this principle through an experiment with 10 grams of solid mercury oxide, which is a red powder. He placed this powder in a sealed container and then heated the container. The powder changed into the silver liquid substance known as mercury. The experiment also produced the gas oxygen. When Lavoisier determined the mass of the oxygen plus the mercury, the product, he found that it was equal to the mass of the mercury oxide, the reactant.

Lavoisier's discovery is considered the basic principle of modern chemistry. It established the balance between reactants and products in chemical equations.

Figure 5.2   The exposure of oxygen to the iron in the frame of this truck has resulted in the formation of rust.

produces heat. This heat causes the sodium to form a rolling molten ball, as well as steam, which is released from the surface of the water. This reaction can be described in the following chemical equation:

$$2Na(s) + 2H_2O(l) \rightarrow 2NaOH(aq) + H_2(g)$$

An example of a Group 2 hydroxide formation is when a small piece of calcium is placed in a test tube of water. When first placed in the water, the calcium sinks to the bottom. At first, there is not much of a reaction. This is because when calcium is exposed to air, a protective oxide coating quickly forms. Eventually, however, this oxide layer is penetrated by the water, causing hydrogen to be released, which produces bubbles that carry the calcium to the surface of the water in the test tube. The bubbles eventually burst,

causing the calcium to sink. However, new bubbles form, pushing the calcium to the surface again. This results in the calcium bobbing up and down in the test tube until all the metal has reacted. Eventually, the calcium-water reaction changes water in the test tube into calcium hydroxide. Because calcium hydroxide is not very soluble, tiny granular particles—or precipitates—form. These precipitates can sink to the bottom of the test tube or remain suspended in the water, giving it a cloudy appearance.

COMBUSTION

Combustion is a chemical reaction that typically occurs when a flame is applied to both a combustible material, such as metal, and a combustible agent, such as oxygen: the reaction produces heat. Compared to other elements in the periodic table, metals take longer to react to the flame and the agent. As more heat is produced, the combustion becomes more intense. If any of the necessary elements—combustible agent, combustible material, or flame—is withdrawn, the combustion ceases, and the fire will go out.

As a substance combusts, it changes and produces new substances. For example, smoke is usually present when there is fire, and soot is usually present when carbon burns. These are new substances that were not present prior to combustion.

A good example of combustion in metals is when sodium reacts with oxygen. For example, if sodium is heated on a spoon until it ignites and is then placed in a dry jar filled with oxygen, it will burn with a bright yellow flame. A solid, sodium peroxide, then forms, as described in the following equation:

$$2Na + O_2 \rightarrow Na_2O_2$$

If the sodium peroxide is then added to water, oxygen and sodium hydroxide form, as follows:

$$2Na_2O_2 + 2H_2O \rightarrow 4NaOH + O_2$$

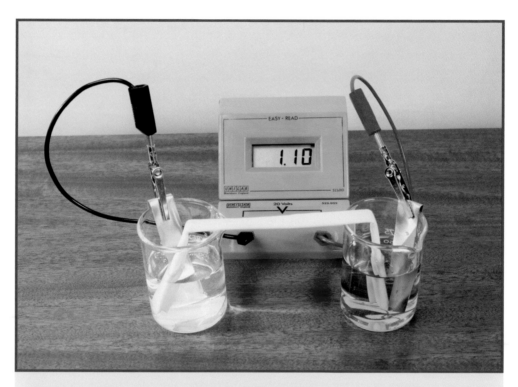

Figure 5.3 **This zinc-copper battery demonstrates electron behavior of the elements zinc and copper. A zinc strip is immersed in sulphuric acid *(left)* and a copper strip is dipped into a copper sulphate solution *(right)*. A "salt bridge" connects the two solutions, closing the circuit and allowing electricity to flow.**

METAL REACTIONS WITH ELECTRICITY

In 1800, Alessandro Volta (1745–1827) invented the world's first battery by using electrolysis to separate water into oxygen and hydrogen. The discovery of electrolysis allowed chemists to isolate metals such as sodium and potassium, and determine certain properties of metals. It also allowed scientists to investigate the chemical reactivity of metals and determine that metals are excellent conductors of electricity.

One chemist, Michael Faraday (1791–1867) discovered that while water was not a good conductor of electricity, its conductivity

improved if salts made from metallic sodium compounds were added. This is because the solution of salt compounds becomes ionized and electricity is carried by ions. Any solution that can transmit electricity is known as an **electrolyte**.

Copper—one of the transition metals—is an excellent conductor of electricity and is often used to build and develop systems that transmit electricity from power stations to homes, offices, and other buildings. Copper is also very ductile, meaning it can be drawn into wires, another factor that makes it ideal for the transmission of electricity. Electricity also makes it possible to apply a thin coating of copper to metals, in the process of electroplating.

ACIDS AND BASES

Metals react with **acids** and **bases**. Acids are chemical compounds that donate hydrogen ions (H^+) to other atoms. Bases are compounds that accept these ions and are often oxides or hydroxides (OH^-). An alkali is a base that can be dissolved in water. Acids and bases react with each other to produce a salt. This reaction typically occurs in a water, or aqueous, solution. The concentration of hydrogen ions in solution is measured on the pH scale. Solutions with pH levels below 7 are acidic, with acidity increasing as the pH decreases. As the pH increases above 7, the solution becomes more basic. A pH of 7 indicates that a solution is neutral.

The pH of a substance can be measured with litmus paper and is called a *litmus test*. When litmus, which is obtained from lichen (organisms that are made up of fungi and another organism that uses photosynthesis to make food for the lichen), is applied to paper, it turns red when it comes into contact with acid. The litmus scale is gradual. As a base neutralizes an acid solution, the color on the litmus paper changes from shades of red to green, and then ultimately to blue. Measurements can range from 1 to 14, with strong acid solutions starting at pH 1 to strong basic solutions measuring pH 14.

When a metal with greater reactivity than hydrogen comes into contact with an acid, the atoms from the metal replace the acid's

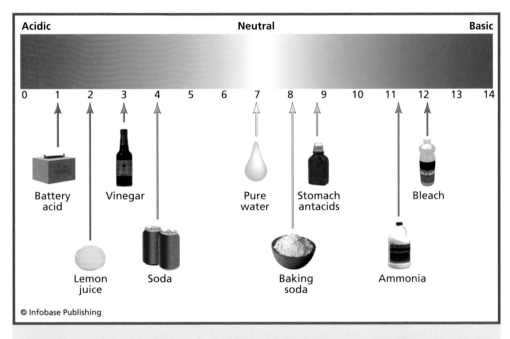

| Acidic | | | | | | | Neutral | | | | | | | Basic |

Battery acid

Vinegar

Lemon juice

Soda

Pure water

Stomach antacids

Baking soda

Ammonia

Bleach

© Infobase Publishing

Figure 5.4 **On a pH scale, 7 represents a neutral substance. Values to the left of 7 indicate solutions that are increasingly acidic. Values to the right indicate an increasingly basic solution.**

hydrogen atoms. The hydrogen is then released as a gas. The solution that remains is a salt. For example, when magnesium combines with hydrochloric acid, the reaction produces hydrogen gas and magnesium chloride, which is a salt compound, as illustrated in this equation:

$$Mg(s) + 2HCl(aq) \rightarrow MgCl_2(aq) + H_2(g)$$

Another example is when sulfuric acid is poured over a piece of zinc. The reaction causes the release of hydrogen gas. The remaining salt solution is composed of zinc sulfate, which bubbles as a result of the reaction. It is important to note, however, that zinc is less reactive than magnesium, so the reaction is not as rapid or vigorous as the reaction between magnesium and hydrochloric acid.

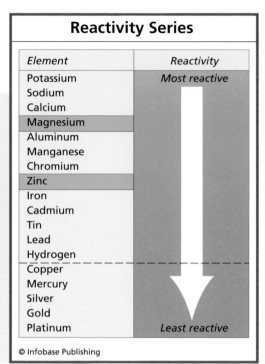

Reactivity Series

Element	Reactivity
Potassium	Most reactive
Sodium	
Calcium	
Magnesium	
Aluminum	
Manganese	
Chromium	
Zinc	
Iron	
Cadmium	
Tin	
Lead	
Hydrogen	
Copper	
Mercury	
Silver	
Gold	
Platinum	Least reactive

© Infobase Publishing

Figure 5.5 The Reactivity Series chart is used to compare the reactivity of elements. Elements higher on the chart are more reactive than elements lower on the chart. For example, sodium is higher on the chart than lead because sodium is more reactive than lead.

SUMMARY

This chapter focused on what happens at the beginning, middle, and end of a chemical reaction, and how metals behave and change during a reaction. There are certain important characteristics of chemical reactions, which are described by chemical equations. For example, there is always a change of energy—either exothermic, when energy is given off as a result of a reaction, or endothermic, when energy is absorbed. There are also various forms of chemical reactions, including oxidation and combustion and those involving electricity and acids and bases.

Metals in Our World

Metals consist of a varied and diverse group of elements. Some metals are found in their pure forms, while others are very reactive and exist in nature only in compounds. Many metals are toxic to living things and dangerous to the environment and need to be closely monitored. But many other metals are vital to our society and our way of life—including the industries where we work, products that we use every day, as well as the building of our homes and our schools. This chapter looks at some common metals and their roles in and impact on our world.

POTASSIUM

Potassium is essential to plant growth. Approximately 95% of mined potassium is used to manufacture the fertilizer potassium nitrate (KNO_3). Potassium is also found in soil, where it is continuously replenished through decaying plants and animal waste.

However, whenever soil is plowed, the nutrient-replenishing process is disrupted and the potassium is lost. This is why it becomes necessary to add fertilizer to soil.

Large amounts of potassium are mined to produce potassium carbonate (K_2CO_3), which is used in glass manufacturing. Adding this compound to glass makes it stronger and more resistant to scratching.

SODIUM

Sodium is present in many compounds that have great economic importance. One of the most well-known compounds is salt, or sodium chloride (NaCl). Approximately 20 million tons of salt is produced every year through the mining of salt deposits all over the world. Salt is also extracted from seawater, although in lower amounts than are available from salt mine deposits.

More than half of the salt produced annually is used by chemical industries to make other compounds, including sodium hydroxide and sodium carbonate. The remainder of the salt produced is used by the food industry as a preservative to prevent foods from spoiling and as a flavoring ingredient. Salt is also used to deice roads during the winter months, when ice and snow can make driving dangerous.

Sodium hydroxide is used in factories, offices, and homes for unblocking clogged drains. Sodium carbonate is used in glassmaking and in the production of detergents. Solutions with sodium carbonate are used to neutralize acid in water. Sodium carbonate is also used to make soft drinks and sodas, because it increases the solubility of carbon dioxide, which gives these drinks their fizzy quality. A related compound, sodium hydrogen carbonate, also known as sodium bicarbonate or baking soda, is used to make fire extinguishers. This compound is combined with sulfuric acid in a pressurized canister to produce carbon dioxide gas, which then produces the foam dispensed by the extinguisher to put out fires. Other important sodium compounds include sodium borohydride

(NaBH$_4$), which bleaches the pulp used to make paper; sodium azide (NaN$_3$), which is used to make air bags in cars; and sodamide (NaNH$_2$), which is used to make dyes.

Sodium is also used for lighting. Sodium gives off a yellow color when it is heated, or when electricity is passed through its vapor. This light does not scatter in fog, which makes sodium ideal for producing street lamps and headlights on automobiles. Bulbs made from sodium also use less electricity.

LITHIUM

Lithium compounds have a number of important industrial uses. Approximately half the lithium oxide produced every year is used to make glass and glass ceramics. This compound, as well as lithium carbonate, is also used in the manufacture of a number of pharmaceutical products.

Lithium is often combined with other metals to form alloys. When combined with aluminum or magnesium, lithium makes the alloys both lighter and stronger. The magnesium-lithium alloy is used to make protective armor plating worn by soldiers and law enforcement officers. The aluminum-lithium alloy is also important to the airline industry. The aircraft made from this alloy are lighter and require less fuel to operate, thus providing a significant cost savings to the airline operators. However, this alloy is more brittle and less ductile than aluminum alone. This problem is resolved through the addition of small amounts of other metals, such as copper or zirconium, to the alloy. Aluminum-magnesium alloys with these metals are also used to make bicycle frames and high-speed trains.

Other important lithium compounds include lithium chloride, which has significant water-absorbing power. This allows for the use of lithium chloride in the manufacture of air conditioning units. Another compound, lithium stearate, is the product of a reaction between stearic acid and lithium hydroxide. This compound is useful as a type of grease able to withstand extremely low temperatures.

LITHIUM AND BOMB MAKING

One of lithium's isotopes—lithium-6—helped scientists during the creation of the hydrogen bomb. In this type of bomb, two hydrogen isotopes, deuterium and tritium, are subjected to thermonuclear **fusion** in order to create an enormous amount of energy. The thermonuclear fusion requires extremely high temperatures—millions of degrees—to combine the isotopes' nuclei. Scientists needed a device that could produce these high temperatures and supply enough of the hydrogen isotopes to make an effective bomb.

During World War II, physicist Edward Teller suggested that a compound using a lithium isotope called lithium-6 and deuterium might work as this device. When this compound, called lithium deuteride, is bombarded with neutrons, it undergoes a nuclear reaction to form tritium. Teller, an American born in Hungary, also suggested surrounding the atom bomb, which was made of uranium, with a layer of lithium deuteride to increase its explosive impact. When the uranium bomb exploded, he explained, the resulting neutron supply would be enough to transform lithium-6 into tritium. The explosion would also produce enough heat to fuse the tritium and the deuterium. Teller's ideas were a success, and the highly destructive bombs were made.

Lithium is also used to store hydrogen. Hydrogen and lithium combine to form lithium hydride. When lithium hydride is combined with water, it releases the hydrogen.

IRON

Iron has more uses and applications than any other metal. With world production of new iron reaching approximately 500 million tons a year, more than 90% of all metal refined is iron. Iron's uses are too numerous to list. From cars to buildings, to ships and

Figure 6.1   **Molten iron is dumped into a furnace as a part of the refining process.**

household appliances, we rely on products made with iron every day of our lives.

Iron is produced by heating iron ore and a form of carbon called *coke* in a blast furnace. The iron oxide in the ore is converted under extremely hot temperatures into molten iron, also known as "pig

iron." Pig iron has to be further transformed, because it is full of impurities such as silicon and manganese, which makes it too brittle to be useful. The pig iron is heated with large amounts of oxygen so that all of the carbon is removed. This process produces steel.

There are many kinds of steel, each of them made by adding a specific product or material to give it a certain property. One example is nickel steel, to which a small amount of nickel has been added to make the resulting product resilient to stress. It is useful for building bridges and utility towers, and for producing bicycle chains. Transition metals, such as tungsten and vanadium, are added to steel to increase its durability at high temperatures. Manganese steel is more durable and resistant to high-energy impact, leading to its use in the production of shovels and rifle barrels. Stainless steel, made by adding nickel and chromium to iron, is often used to produce cookware.

Iron has also played an important role in warfare and weaponry. Beginning in the Iron Age, around 1100 B.C., warriors began to use iron swords. These powerful swords vanquished many opponents and were the weapon of choice for more than 2,000 years. Later in history, iron also played a role in the production of gunpowder, cannonballs, gun shells, and bullets.

URANIUM

Uranium is the heaviest natural element. It produces enormous energy and is used to make atomic bombs and nuclear reactors. It is so powerful—and so dangerous in the wrong hands—that the United States government has established a special agency called the Nuclear Regulatory Commission whose job is to control all buying or selling of uranium,.

There are three primary isotopes of uranium: uranium-238, uranium-235, and uranium-234. These isotopes have incredibly long half-lives. Uranium-238 has the longest half-life—4.6 billion years. This means that the isotope is less radioactive because fewer of its nuclei disintegrate. Uranium-235 has a half-life of 700 million

years, whereas the half-life of uranium-234 is 25 million years. Because these half-lives are so long, pure uranium's radioactivity is considered fairly weak. When pure uranium begins to decay, other radioactive isotopes begin to form, including radon and polonium. These isotopes are known as the uranium decay series.

During the 1930s, scientists discovered a process known as nuclear **fission** through experiments with uranium. They noticed that when they bombarded uranium with neutrons, two elements were produced—barium and krypton—whose atoms were about half the size of a uranium atom. The scientists determined that the uranium nucleus was splitting into two fragments through a process they called nuclear fission. Along with the splitting of the nucleus, a number of neutrons were released, as well as a significant amount of energy. Scientists used the results of these discoveries to split a chain of uranium nuclei, which produces the energy that currently comes from nuclear reactors. In a controlled environment, this energy can be used in power plants. In an uncontrolled chain reaction, uranium produces an atomic explosion. Uranium was a key element in the first atomic bomb ever used in warfare. The bomb, which contained the isotope uranium-235, was dropped on the Japanese city of Hiroshima on August 6, 1945, during World War II. Its blast was powerful enough to destroy almost 50,000 buildings and kill about 75,000 people.

SILVER

Silver is widely used for a variety of commercial and industrial purposes. American industries use more than 6 million pounds (2.7 million kg) of silver every year. Almost 25% of this amount is used by the electronics industry, although the photography industry also uses a significant amount to make photographic film and paper. The dental supply industry also uses silver to make cavity fillings for teeth.

Compounds that contain silver—such as silver chloride, silver iodide, and silver bromide—are highly sensitive to light. When

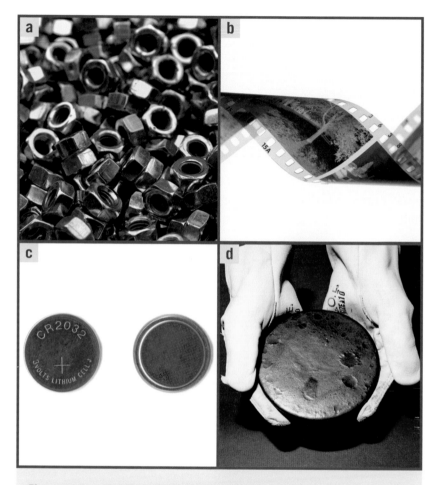

Figure 6.2   Metals are used in a variety of applications: (a) zinc nuts; (b) photographic film; (c) a lithium battery; (d) a piece of uranium called a billet.

exposed to light, these silver salts darken, a process known as photochemical decomposition. Photographic film includes an emulsion made from silver bromide. When the light hits this emulsion, the silver ions in the silver bromide molecule become "excited." These charged ions form atoms on the surface of the emulsion while reproducing the photographed image on the film. Silver salts

are also used to make photochromic sunglasses, which darken in sunlight. Small grains of silver chloride are combined with glass in the manufacture of these lenses. When the surface of the lens is exposed to light, a thin layer of silver develops on the glass. Once out of the light, the lenses become clear again due to the addition of copper ions, which cause the silver ions to revert to their original form.

ZINC

Approximately 90% of the zinc produced in the United States is used in the production of galvanized steel. Galvanization involves coating steel with a layer of zinc in order to protect it from reacting with the air, which can cause the steel to corrode. Common household objects and commercial products, including trash cans and metal fencing, are made out of galvanized steel.

Zinc is also used to make batteries. In fact, the first dry battery produced used a zinc anode, a carbon cathode, and an alkaline electrolyte made from ammonium chloride paste to deliver 1.5 volts of energy.

Zinc is used in coin-making. Beginning in the early 1980s, zinc—instead of copper—has been used to manufacture pennies, though a thin top layer of copper is still used to give pennies a reddish-brown appearance. A zinc compound—zinc sulfide—is used as a **phosphor** in the production of many electronic devices. Phosphors, which give off light when struck with electrons, are used to coat tubes inside televisions and computer monitors. After an electron-filled beam is generated in the tube, it strikes the zinc sulfide coating, and then produces the picture or computer images seen on the screen.

Another important commercial compound is zinc oxide, which is used as a catalyst in the rubber industry and to make pigment for products such as plastics, cosmetics, wallpaper, and printing inks. This compound also conducts electricity and is used to make photocopying machines.

MERCURY

Mercury is a volatile, toxic substance. It is easily absorbed into the body through the skin or by inhalation, and it goes on to chemically combine with the body's enzymes, causing them to lose any ability to perform their job as catalysts. Symptoms of mercury poisoning include deterioration of basic nervous system functions, such as loss of nerve reflexes and motor skills. Loss of teeth or hair can also occur, as well as memory damage. It does not take a significant amount of mercury to do harm. In fact, experts estimate that vapors from a teaspoon of mercury can contaminate a fairly large room within a week and make it unsafe for humans. For these reasons, mercury is extremely hazardous to those chemists who use it in experiments. Great care is needed when handling mercury.

Although it is dangerous to humans, mercury is a most effective poison for dealing with insect pests. For example, mercuric chloride ($HgCl_2$) is an effective fungicide and pesticide. A similar compound, mercurous chloride (Hg_2Cl_2), is not as toxic as mercuric chloride and is used in the agriculture industry to control maggots and other pests that can damage crops.

However, the use of mercury as a pesticide and insecticide has had a negative effect on the environment, and many compounds that contain mercury have been banned from use in commercial and agricultural industries. When used in agriculture, mercury eventually makes its way to water sources such as lakes and rivers. Certain microorganisms that live in these water bodies can metabolize mercury. Fish, such as salmon and swordfish, rely on these microorganisms as a staple of their diet. If these microorganisms are contaminated by mercury, the fish will also become contaminated. Scientists and health experts are concerned that the mercury will accumulate in large fish, such as salmon, that are sold as food, which can in turn cause dangerous levels of this metal to build up in humans. Efforts are currently under way to halt contamination of water sources by mercury-containing compounds.

MAGNESIUM

Magnesium is an important structural material, primarily because of its low density. With a density of 1.74 g/cm^3, magnesium is only slightly denser than water, which has a density of 1.00 g/cm^3. The density of magnesium is about one-fifth that of iron and two-thirds that of aluminum. Typically, magnesium is mixed with other metals to form alloys that are light and strong. When aluminum and magnesium are combined, the alloy is lighter and more resistant to corrosion than aluminum alone, and it is also durable enough to withstand heavy use. The aluminum-magnesium alloy is used to make household products such as ladders, as well as power tools, aircraft parts, and racing bikes. Magnesium and its alloys are also used by automobile manufacturers because of their low-density properties, which allow them to manufacture lighter-weight vehicles. Lighter vehicles benefit the environment, in turn, because they use less fuel, last longer, and they also cause less damage in car accidents. When these products reach the end of their usefulness, the magnesium can be recycled at low cost.

In the natural world, magnesium plays an important role in the life cycle of all green plants. Magnesium is present in chlorophyll, which converts solar energy to chemical energy through photosynthesis. Magnesium provides the chlorophyll molecule with its ability to absorb light, as well as the molecule's green color.

SUMMARY

This chapter examined where metals come from and how they behave in their natural environment. Many of the metals mentioned here play a significant role in our daily lives, and help to make products that we used every day. For example, sodium chloride (NaCl), or salt, is a key flavoring agent for the food supply. Sodium carbonate, another sodium substance, is used not only in glassmaking and to make light fixtures, but also to produce cleaning materials like detergents. Our homes and schools would likely

not exist without iron, which has a wider range of uses than any other metal, including its use in the production of building materials like steel. Some metals, like mercury, have toxic characteristics, which are important to learn about before working with them in a classroom or laboratory setting.

Metals and Our Bodies and Health

Our bodies interact with metallic elements every day. Some metal elements are present in our body, whereas others are used to make medicines that keep us healthy. Other metals, such as mercury, are dangerous to human health. This chapter examines how some of these elements interact with our bodies.

POTASSIUM AND SODIUM IN THE HUMAN BODY

Both potassium and sodium play a key role in how our bodies transmit impulses and messages throughout the nervous system. There are two kinds of fluid in the body: **intracellular (ICF)** and **extracellular (ECF)**. ICF, the fluid within the cells, contains 65% of the body's total water. ECF, the fluid outside the cells, contains the remaining 35%. ECF is composed of a sodium and chloride solution, NaCl, which breaks down to become sodium cations (Na^+) and chlorine anions (Cl^-). ICF is composed of potassium

cations (K^+). Both Na^+ and K^+ are essential for neurons to conduct impulses throughout the body.

Potassium

Red blood cells, muscles, and brain tissue all need potassium. The body's lean tissues and kidneys also need a constant supply of potassium to function properly. People who are potassium deficient could experience muscle weakness, which can adversely affect the heart muscles. This can lead to the development of an irregular heartbeat and possibly even cardiac arrest. Certain medical conditions can cause potassium deficiency, such as starvation and certain kidney diseases. Diarrhea can cause a significant loss of potassium, causing symptoms of weakness and exhaustion. Because there is so much potassium in foods such as fruits and vegetables, however, chronic potassium deficiency is rare.

Too much potassium, however, is also bad for the body. Several grams of the compound potassium chloride can actually paralyze the nervous system. The presence of too much potassium disrupts the transmission of electrical impulses. This causes all body functions to shut down, including the heart muscles, which will eventually stop beating altogether.

Sodium

Sodium is required in animal and human diets. A deficiency in sodium can result in muscle spasms. However, too much sodium in a diet can have a negative effect on health. Doctors advise patients with heart or kidney disease to decrease the amount of sodium in their diet. If the heart or kidneys are not functioning properly, the body's ability to eliminate excess sodium is diminished. The body compensates by retaining water, which causes pressure to increase on the arteries. This increased pressure leads to numerous health problems, including high blood pressure.

In tropical climates, salt is a lifesaver. Diarrhea is common among children living in these areas, and it can cause dehydration

if the child goes untreated. In fact, there are some estimates that diarrhea and dehydration kill more than 10 million children a year. One simple, inexpensive treatment is a glucose and salt solution. Made of glucose, sodium citrate, and potassium chloride, these ingredients are dissolved in water for drinking by children or adults. This solution is also effective against the diarrhea caused by another tropical disease called *cholera.*

Iron in the Human Body

Iron is especially important to the human body because it transports oxygen to the organs and tissues. Oxygen is carried in red blood cells by a molecule called **hemoglobin**. Each hemoglobin molecule contains four iron atoms. The oxygen molecules bind to the hemoglobin's iron atoms and travel throughout the body.

In addition to its role in transporting oxygen, iron has many other roles in the human body. Iron is important for the function of various enzymes, and allows cells to use glucose to release energy. Certain areas of the brain contain significant amounts of iron, which indicates that this metal is needed for normal brain function. Some researchers theorize that iron deficiency in infants and young children can slow mental development. The liver is also rich in iron. In fact, this organ stores excess amounts of the metal.

Iron is lost through the intestine walls and because of this the human body needs to take in a certain amount of iron every day. The recommended daily iron intake for men is around 7 milligrams. Women need slightly more, about 11 milligrams. In the Western world, both men and women can easily obtain enough iron through a normal diet. In fact, a typical Western diet provides about 20 milligrams of iron each day, because many diet staples, such as bread and eggs, are rich in iron. Not all the iron contained in food is absorbed by the body—in fact, only about 25% is. But this is enough to satisfy the body's daily needs.

While the Western world gets plenty of iron through diet, iron-deficient diets are a problem for many people in the rest of the

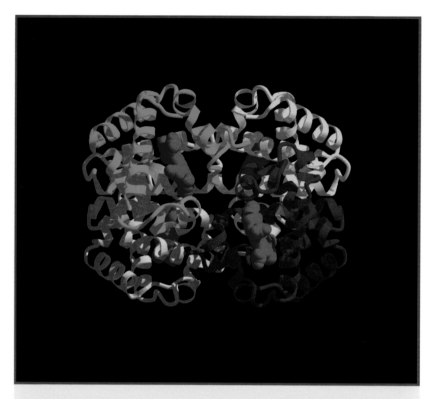

Figure 7.1 This photograph shows the ribbon structure of a hemoglobin molecule. Hemoglobin, found in blood, helps the body transport oxygen. The red color of blood comes from the iron in hemoglobin.

world. Iron deficiency can lead to a condition known as **anemia**. It is estimated that, worldwide, approximately 500 million people are anemic because they do not get enough iron in their diet. Symptoms of anemia include tiredness, dizziness, and sometimes a rapid heartbeat.

The presence of too much iron in the body can also cause problems. People who suffer from hemochromatosis retain too much iron, causing it to accumulate in various organs, including the spleen, heart, and liver. Hemochromatosis can cause joint pain, heart failure, liver failure, or diabetes.

MERCURY IN THE HUMAN BODY

Pure mercury and compounds that contain mercury are toxic to humans. Because mercury is absorbed through the lungs, skin, and digestive system, any exposure to the metal poses a danger of mercury poisoning. Pregnant women and their unborn babies are vulnerable to mercury poisoning. If a pregnant woman is exposed to mercury and it enters her body, it can pass into the placenta and harm the fetus.

Initial symptoms of mercury poisoning include severe headaches, nausea, vomiting, stomach pains, and diarrhea. Repeated exposure to mercury over long periods causes it to build up in the body, leading to more severe symptoms, including excessive

MEASURING MERCURY IN HAIR

The level of mercury that has accumulated in a person's body over a lifetime can be measured through a strand of hair. Sulfur attracts mercury, and hair is composed of many different kinds of sulfur-containing amino acids. These substances attract mercury and create a permanent record of a person's lifetime exposure to the metal. In earlier times, it was common for families and friends to save a lock of hair from someone who passed away. Using modern technology, hairs from various periods in history have been analyzed for mercury levels. For example, hair from the famous scientist Sir Isaac Newton (1642–1727) was found to contain high levels of mercury. This is not surprising, since he worked with chemicals most of his life and was probably exposed to significant amounts of mercury. England's King Charles II was also found to have high levels of mercury in his hair after he died. Charles practiced alchemy, and was likely exposed to high levels of the metal in poorly ventilated rooms.

salivating, swollen salivary glands, and loosening of the teeth. Eventually, mercury poisoning affects the brain and other areas of the central nervous system, causing fatigue, weakness, memory loss, and sleep disorders. Psychological symptoms are also common, including depression, paranoia, and irritability.

In the past, certain occupations posed a particular risk of mercury poisoning. During the nineteenth century, the phrase "mad as a hatter"—which was popularized by the Mad Hatter character in Lewis Carroll's *Alice in Wonderland*—comes from the former practice of hat makers using mercury compounds in the production of certain kinds of hats. These hat makers, or hatters, were known to exhibit unusual behavior, including slurred speech and tremors, and were often irritable, depressed, and paranoid, which was eventually traced to mercury poisoning. Hatters worked for long hours in poorly ventilated rooms, which only increased the hatters' chronic exposure to mercury. In the mid-twentieth century, many countries outlawed the use of mercury compounds in the hat-making industries. In the twentieth century, many detectives and law enforcement officials used a mercury compound to dust for fingerprints at crime scenes, until it was understood to be dangerous. Today, there are different substances used in fingerprint-detecting powders, including aluminum and zinc.

CALCIUM IN THE HUMAN BODY

Calcium is essential to all living things. Calcium compounds are a vital component of the skeletons and bones of mammals, amphibians, reptiles, birds, fish, and other land and marine animals. The most abundant metal in the human body, calcium makes up the bones and serves other functions in the body's metabolic system. These functions include keeping cells joined together, aiding in muscle contraction and conduction of nerve impulses, helping blood clot, and controlling cell division.

Because calcium is so important in keeping the human body functioning properly, it is an important component of the daily diet of all people. It is especially important for children and pregnant

Figure 7.2   Calcium is found in many foods. A diet rich in calcium promotes good health, including healthy teeth, bones, and nerve impulses.

women because it promotes the growth and health of bones and teeth. Foods rich in calcium include cheese, milk, yogurt, and leafy greens such as spinach.

Calcium and calcium-containing compounds have been used frequently in various medicines. For example, calcium carbonate is an effective antacid for indigestion, and calcium lactate can be used to help calcium deficiency.

ZINC IN THE HUMAN BODY

Zinc is essential to the health of both humans and animals. The body stores zinc primarily in the eyes, muscles, kidneys, and liver. The body loses about 1% of its total amount of zinc every day, primarily through sweat and urine. In addition, zinc is important

to the body's enzymes that regulate growth, development, and longevity. Zinc-containing enzymes also help the body's digestive and immune systems to work properly, and they are known to be involved in the parts of the brain that regulate taste and smell. The average adult takes in between 5 and 40 milligrams of zinc every day. Foods rich in zinc include beef, liver, lamb, and cheese.

LITHIUM IN THE HUMAN BODY

Lithium has various medicinal uses, though at certain levels it can be toxic. In the nineteenth century, lithium was used as a treatment for gout, a painful condition where uric acid builds up around certain joints, particularly around the feet. As uric acid builds up, its molecules form crystals. These crystallized molecules are fairly insoluble, which can hamper treatment. However, doctors discovered that if lithium was incorporated into the uric acid compounds, the compound was more soluble, and thus easier to dissolve. Bathing in lithium-rich springs and spas soon became popular for treating gout. Unfortunately, it was discovered that the lithium was too diluted in these spa waters to have any beneficial effect.

In the mid-1900s, doctors conducted experiments with patients suffering from depression, treating them with various lithium compounds. By the 1970s, lithium was commonly used in Europe and the United States to treat patients with manic depression, which is characterized by extreme mood swings. It is not clear exactly how lithium works to help patients. Some researchers believe that manic depression involves the overproduction of a chemical in the brain called *inositol phosphate*, and that lithium works to normalize levels of this chemical.

SUMMARY

Throughout this volume of the *Essential Chemistry* series, we learned how metals are important to the environment and to our bodies. But this is a rich subject, and this book is only a beginning exploration into a specific group of elements. To help you

learn more about metals, the final pages of this book contain suggestions for further reading and recommended Web sites for browsing. These resources will guide you to a deeper education and understanding of metals, as well as the other elements of the periodic table.

PERIODIC TABLE OF THE ELEMENTS

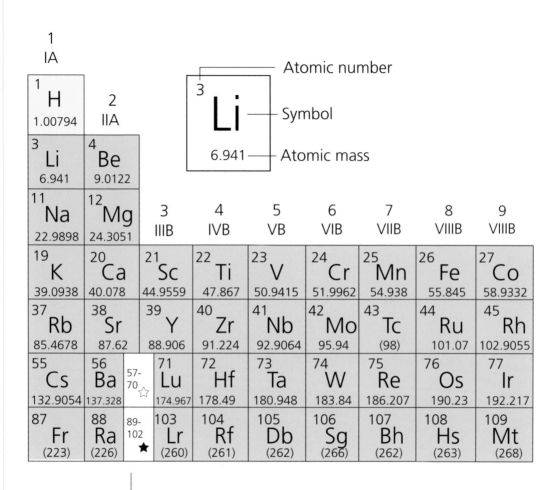

Numbers in parentheses are atomic mass numbers of most stable isotopes.

Metals

Non-metals

Metalloids

			13 IIIA	14 IVA	15 VA	16 VIA	17 VIIA	18 VIIIA
								2 He 4.0026
			5 B 10.81	6 C 12.011	7 N 14.0067	8 O 15.9994	9 F 18.9984	10 Ne 20.1798
10 VIIIB	11 IB	12 IIB	13 Al 26.9815	14 Si 28.0855	15 P 30.9738	16 S 32.067	17 Cl 35.4528	18 Ar 39.948
28 Ni 58.6934	29 Cu 63.546	30 Zn 65.409	31 Ga 69.723	32 Ge 72.61	33 As 74.9216	34 Se 78.96	35 Br 79.904	36 Kr 83.798
46 Pd 106.42	47 Ag 107.8682	48 Cd 112.412	49 In 114.818	50 Sn 118.711	51 Sb 121.760	52 Te 127.60	53 I 126.9045	54 Xe 131.29
78 Pt 195.08	79 Au 196.9655	80 Hg 200.59	81 Tl 204.3833	82 Pb 207.2	83 Bi 208.9804	84 Po (209)	85 At (210)	86 Rn (222)
110 Ds (271)	111 Rg (272)	112 Uub (277)						

62 Sm 150.36	63 Eu 151.966	64 Gd 157.25	65 Tb 158.9253	66 Dy 162.500	67 Ho 164.9303	68 Er 167.26	69 Tm 168.9342	70 Yb 173.04
94 Pu (244)	95 Am 243	96 Cm (247)	97 Bk (247)	98 Cf (251)	99 Es (252)	100 Fm (257)	101 Md (258)	102 No (259)

ELECTRON CONFIGURATIONS

Atomic number — 3
Symbol — Li
Electron configuration — $[He]\ 2s^1$

1 IA ns^1	2 ns^2	3 IIIB	4 IVB	5 VB	6 VIB	7 VIIB	8 VIIIB	9 VIIIB
1 H $1s^1$								
3 Li $[He]2s^1$	4 Be $[He]2s^2$							
11 Na $[Ne]3s^1$	12 Mg $[Ne]3s^2$							
19 K $[Ar]4s^1$	20 Ca $[Ar]\ 4s^2$	21 Sc $[Ar]4s^23d^1$	22 Ti $[Ar]4s^23d^2$	23 V $[Ar]4s^23d^3$	24 Cr $[Ar]4s^13d^5$	25 Mn $[Ar]4s^23d^5$	26 Fe $[Ar]4s^23d^6$	27 Co $[Ar]4s^23d^7$
37 Rb $[Kr]5s^1$	38 Sr $[Kr]5s^2$	39 Y $[Kr]5s^24d^1$	40 Zr $[Kr]5s^24d^2$	41 Nb $[Kr]5s^14d^4$	42 Mo $[Kr]5s^14d^5$	43 Tc $[Kr]5s^14d^6$	44 Ru $[Kr]5s^14d^7$	45 Rh $[Kr]5s^14d^8$
55 Cs $[Xe]6s^1$	56 Ba $[Xe]6s^2$	57-70 ☆; 71 Lu $[Xe]6s^24f^{14}5d^1$	72 Hf $[Xe]4f^{14}6s^25d^2$	73 Ta $[Xe]6s^25d^3$	74 W $[Xe]6s^25d^4$	75 Re $[Xe]6s^25d^5$	76 Os $[Xe]6s^25d^6$	77 Ir $[Xe]6s^25d^7$
87 Fr $[Rn]7s^1$	88 Ra $[Rn]7s^2$	89-102 ★; 103 Lr $[Rn]7s^25f^{14}6d^1$	104 Rf $[Rn]7s^26d^2$	105 Db $[Rn]7s^26d^3$	106 Sg $[Rn]7s^26d^4$	107 Bh $[Rn]7s^26d^5$	108 Hs $[Rn]7s^26d^6$	109 Mt $[Rn]7s^26d^7$

☆ Lanthanides

★ Actinides

57 La $[Xe]6s^25d^1$	58 Ce $[Xe]6s^24f^15d^1$	59 Pr $[Xe]6s^24f^35d^0$	60 Nd $[Xe]6s^24f^45d^0$	61 Pm $[Xe]6s^24f^55d^0$
89 Ac $[Rn]7s^26d^1$	90 Th $[Rn]7s^25f^06d^2$	91 Pa $[Rn]7s^25f^26d^1$	92 U $[Rn]7s^25f^36d^1$	93 Np $[Rn]7s^25f^46d^1$

							18 VIIIA ns^2np^6
	13 IIIA ns^2np^1	14 IVA ns^2np^2	15 VA ns^2np^3	16 VIA ns^2np^4	17 VIIA ns^2np^5		2 He $1s^2$

10 VIIB	11 IB	12 IIB	13 IIIA ns^2np^1	14 IVA ns^2np^2	15 VA ns^2np^3	16 VIA ns^2np^4	17 VIIA ns^2np^5	18 VIIIA ns^2np^6
			5 B $[He]2s^22p^1$	6 C $[He]2s^22p^2$	7 N $[He]2s^22p^3$	8 O $[He]2s^22p^4$	9 F $[He]2s^22p^5$	10 Ne $[He]2s^22p^6$
			13 Al $[Ne]3s^23p^1$	14 Si $[Ne]3s^23p^2$	15 P $[Ne]3s^23p^3$	16 S $[Ne]3s^23p^4$	17 Cl $[Ne]3s^23p^5$	18 Ar $[Ne]3s^23p^6$
28 Ni $[Ar]4s^23d^8$	29 Cu $[Ar]4s^13d^{10}$	30 Zn $[Ar]4s^23d^{10}$	31 Ga $[Ar]4s^24p^1$	32 Ge $[Ar]4s^24p^2$	33 As $[Ar]4s^24p^3$	34 Se $[Ar]4s^24p^4$	35 Br $[Ar]4s^24p^5$	36 Kr $[Ar]4s^24p^6$
46 Pd $[Kr]4d^{10}$	47 Ag $[Kr]5s^14d^{10}$	48 Cd $[Kr]5s^24d^{10}$	49 In $[Kr]5s^25p^1$	50 Sn $[Kr]5s^25p^2$	51 Sb $[Kr]5s^25p^3$	52 Te $[Kr]5s^25p^4$	53 I $[Kr]5s^25p^5$	54 Xe $[Kr]5s^25p^6$
78 Pt $[Xe]6s^15d^9$	79 Au $[Xe]6s^15d^{10}$	80 Hg $[Xe]6s^25d^{10}$	81 Tl $[Xe]6s^26p^1$	82 Pb $[Xe]6s^26p^2$	83 Bi $[Xe]6s^26p^3$	84 Po $[Xe]6s^26p^4$	85 At $[Xe]6s^26p^5$	86 Rn $[Xe]6s^26p^6$
110 Ds $[Rn]7s^16d^9$	111 Rg $[Rn]7s^16d^{10}$	112 Uub $[Rn]7s^26d^{10}$						

62 Sm [Xe] $6s^24f^65d^0$	63 Eu [Xe] $6s^24f^75d^0$	64 Gd [Xe] $6s^24f^75d^1$	65 Tb [Xe] $6s^24f^95d^0$	66 Dy [Xe] $6s^24f^{10}5d^0$	67 Ho [Xe] $6s^24f^{11}5d^0$	68 Er [Xe] $6s^24f^{12}5d^0$	69 Tm [Xe] $6s^24f^{13}5d^0$	70 Yb [Xe] $6s^24f^{14}5d^0$
94 Pu [Rn] $7s^25f^66d^0$	95 Am [Rn] $7s^25f^76d^0$	96 Cm [Rn] $7s^25f^76d^1$	97 Bk [Rn] $7s^25f^96d^0$	98 Cf [Rn] $7s^25f^{10}6d^0$	99 Es [Rn] $7s^25f^{11}6d^0$	100 Fm [Rn] $7s^25f^{12}6d^0$	101 Md [Rn] $7s^25f^{13}6d^0$	102 No [Rn] $7s^25f^{14}6d^1$

TABLE OF ATOMIC MASSES

ELEMENT	SYMBOL	ATOMIC NUMBER	ATOMIC MASS	ELEMENT	SYMBOL	ATOMIC NUMBER	ATOMIC MASS
Actinium	Ac	89	(227)	Francium	Fr	87	(223)
Aluminum	Al	13	26.9815	Gadolinium	Gd	64	157.25
Americium	Am	95	243	Gallium	Ga	31	69.723
Antimony	Sb	51	121.76	Germanium	Ge	32	72.61
Argon	Ar	18	39.948	Gold	Au	79	196.9655
Arsenic	As	33	74.9216	Hafnium	Hf	72	178.49
Astatine	At	85	(210)	Hassium	Hs	108	(263)
Barium	Ba	56	137.328	Helium	He	2	4.0026
Berkelium	Bk	97	(247)	Holmium	Ho	67	164.9303
Beryllium	Be	4	9.0122	Hydrogen	H	1	1.00794
Bismuth	Bi	83	208.9804	Indium	In	49	114.818
Bohrium	Bh	107	(262)	Iodine	I	53	126.9045
Boron	B	5	10.81	Iridium	Ir	77	192.217
Bromine	Br	35	79.904	Iron	Fe	26	55.845
Cadmium	Cd	48	112.412	Krypton	Kr	36	83.798
Calcium	Ca	20	40.078	Lanthanum	La	57	138.9055
Californium	Cf	98	(251)	Lawrencium	Lr	103	(260)
Carbon	C	6	12.011	Lead	Pb	82	207.2
Cerium	Ce	58	140.115	Lithium	Li	3	6.941
Cesium	Cs	55	132.9054	Lutetium	Lu	71	174.967
Chlorine	Cl	17	35.4528	Magnesium	Mg	12	24.3051
Chromium	Cr	24	51.9962	Manganese	Mn	25	54.938
Cobalt	Co	27	58.9332	Meitnerium	Mt	109	(268)
Copper	Cu	29	63.546	Mendelevium	Md	101	(258)
Curium	Cm	96	(247)	Mercury	Hg	80	200.59
Darmstadtium	Ds	110	(271)	Molybdenum	Mo	42	95.94
Dubnium	Db	105	(262)	Neodymium	Nd	60	144.24
Dysprosium	Dy	66	162.5	Neon	Ne	10	20.1798
Einsteinium	Es	99	(252)	Neptunium	Np	93	(237)
Erbium	Er	68	167.26	Nickel	Ni	28	58.6934
Europium	Eu	63	151.966	Niobium	Nb	41	92.9064
Fermium	Fm	100	(257)	Nitrogen	N	7	14.0067
Fluorine	F	9	18.9984	Nobelium	No	102	(259)

ELEMENT	SYMBOL	ATOMIC NUMBER	ATOMIC MASS
Osmium	Os	76	190.23
Oxygen	O	8	15.9994
Palladium	Pd	46	106.42
Phosphorus	P	15	30.9738
Platinum	Pt	78	195.08
Plutonium	Pu	94	(244)
Polonium	Po	84	(209)
Potassium	K	19	39.0938
Praseodymium	Pr	59	140.908
Promethium	Pm	61	(145)
Protactinium	Pa	91	231.036
Radium	Ra	88	(226)
Radon	Rn	86	(222)
Rhenium	Re	75	186.207
Rhodium	Rh	45	102.9055
Roentgenium	Rg	111	(272)
Rubidium	Rb	37	85.4678
Ruthenium	Ru	44	101.07
Rutherfordium	Rf	104	(261)
Samarium	Sm	62	150.36
Scandium	Sc	21	44.9559
Seaborgium	Sg	106	(266)
Selenium	Se	34	78.96

ELEMENT	SYMBOL	ATOMIC NUMBER	ATOMIC MASS
Silicon	Si	14	28.0855
Silver	Ag	47	107.8682
Sodium	Na	11	22.9898
Strontium	Sr	38	87.62
Sulfur	S	16	32.067
Tantalum	Ta	73	180.948
Technetium	Tc	43	(98)
Tellurium	Te	52	127.6
Terbium	Tb	65	158.9253
Thallium	Tl	81	204.3833
Thorium	Th	90	232.0381
Thulium	Tm	69	168.9342
Tin	Sn	50	118.711
Titanium	Ti	22	47.867
Tungsten	W	74	183.84
Ununbium	Uub	112	(277)
Uranium	U	92	238.0289
Vanadium	V	23	50.9415
Xenon	Xe	54	131.29
Ytterbium	Yb	70	173.04
Yttrium	Y	39	88.906
Zinc	Zn	30	65.409
Zirconium	Zr	40	91.224

GLOSSARY

Acids Substances that yield hydrogen ions when dissolved in water; these substances also accept electron pairs to form covalent bonds.

Actinides Elements 89 through 103 in the periodic table.

Alchemy A science practiced during the Middle Ages and Renaissance that involved efforts to turn metals into gold.

Alkali metals The elements in Group 1 of the periodic table.

Alkaline earth metals The elements that make up Group 2 of the periodic table.

Alloy A physical mixture of two or more metals.

Amalgams Alloys of mercury and other metals, such as tin or silver.

Analysis The process of studying the basic elements of a substance.

Anemia Blood disorder caused by iron deficiency.

Anion An ion with a negative charge.

Anode A terminal on an electrical device from which electrons flow toward an electrical circuit.

Atomic mass The average mass of the atoms in an element.

Atomic number The number of protons in an atom's nucleus.

Atoms The smallest unit of an element, made up of protons, electrons, and neutrons.

Base A compound that reacts with an acid to form a salt; also an ion with a free pair of electrons that can be donated to an acid.

Catalyst An element that accelerates a chemical reaction while remaining unchanged.

Cathode Opposite of an anode; a terminal on an electrical device from which electrons or an electrical current leave or exit a cell or tube.

Cation An ion with a positive charge.

Chemical reaction   A transformation process in which a substance decomposes, combines with other substances, or exchanges electrons with other substances.

Chlorophyll   Any of a group of green pigments in plants that are needed for photosynthesis.

Coefficient   A numerical unit of measure used to describe relative amounts of elements or compounds.

Compound   A substance made up of two or more elements.

Corrosion   A process by which metals are eroded through exposure to oxygen.

Density   The compact property of a substance; also the mass per unit volume of a substance.

Dipole   The separation of both positive and negative electrical charges, or polarities, of equal magnitude in a molecule.

Distillation   A process of purifying mixtures by evaporation of the liquid into gas through heating, and then subsequent condensation of gas to liquid through cooling.

Ductile   A characteristic of metallic elements that allows them to be drawn into wires.

Electrolysis   A process by which an electrical current is passed through a substance to break a chemical bond.

Electrolyte   A chemical compound or ion that is able to conduct electricity in water.

Electrons   Negatively charged particles that orbit the nucleus of an atom.

Electroplating   To coat or plate with a metallic substance through electrolysis.

Element   A substance that cannot be broken down into a simpler form by ordinary chemical or physical means.

Endothermic   A chemical reaction that involves the absorption of heat.

Enzymes   Proteins produced by living cells that act as catalysts for initiating chemical reactions in organisms.

Exothermic   A chemical reaction that involves the release of heat.

Extracellular fluid (ECF)   Fluid outside the body's cells.

Fission   The process of splitting something into two parts; nuclear fission involves splitting an atomic nucleus into smaller fragments.

Fusion   The process of unifying various elements or compounds; nuclear fusion is when nuclei from lighter atoms join together to form the nuclei of heavier atoms.

Half-life   The time it takes for half of the atoms of a substance to disintegrate.

Hemoglobin   The molecule in red blood cells that carries oxygen throughout the body.

Intracellular fluid (ICF)   Fluid within the body's cells.

Ion   An atom or molecule with an electrical charge.

Ionic bond   A bond that is formed when one or more electrons are transferred between two ions of opposite charges.

Isotope   A form of a chemical element that has the same number of protons in the nucleus, but a different numbers of neutrons and therefore a different atomic mass.

Lanthanides   Also called rare earth elements, these appear as elements 57 through 71 on the periodic table.

Magnetism   The attraction or repulsion property of some elements.

Malleable   The ability of a substance, such as a metal, to be hammered or rolled into sheets.

Metals   A class of chemical elements, including gold, copper, silver, and tin. Metals are good conductors of electricity.

Mineral   A naturally occurring substance that has a uniform composition and structure; they are typically mined and some have commercial value.

Neurotransmitter   Chemical substance in the body that is involved in transmitting nerve impulses; examples include epinephrine and acetylcholine.

Neutron   Particle with a neutral charge located in the atom's nucleus.

Noble gases   Six elements located in Group 18 of the periodic table; these elements are very stable and do not form compounds readily.

Nucleus   The core of an atom, made up of protons and neutrons.

Oxidation   The chemical combination of a substance with oxygen.

Periodic table   A chart of the chemical elements; the elements are organized into groups and periods according to similar behaviors and composition.

Phosphors   Compounds that give off light when struck by a beam of electrons.

Photosynthesis   The process by which green plants, algae, and some kinds of bacteria produce carbohydrates from carbon dioxide and water. Chlorophyll captures and stores energy for the process. Oxygen is released as a byproduct of the process.

Products   Substances that form as a result of a chemical reaction.

Protons   Positively charged particles located in the atom's nucleus.

Radioactive   Term used to describe materials that have unstable nuclei capable of spontaneously emitting particles, nucleons, electrons, and gamma rays if the nuclei disintegrate.

Reactants   Substances that undergo change or transformation through a chemical reaction.

Rust   Orange, reddish substance that forms on the surface of iron after exposure to air and moisture.

Superoxides   Metals that form highly reactive compounds with oxygen. When they come into contact with water or carbon dioxide, they cause the release of oxygen.

Synthesis   The forming of complex compounds or substances from elements or simpler compounds.

Tarnish   The discoloration of a metal's surface due to oxidation.

Transition metals   The elements located in the center of the periodic table (Groups 3–12).

BIBLIOGRAPHY

Beatty, Richard. *The Elements: Copper*. New York: Benchmark Books, 2001.

Biology Daily: The Biology Encyclopedia. "Friedrich Strohmeyer," Available online. URL: http://www.biologydaily.com/biology/Friedrich_Strohmeyer.

Challoner, Jack. *The Visual Dictionary of Chemistry*. New York: DK Publishing, 1996.

Chemical Heritage Foundation. "Salt: The First Antibiotic," Available online. URL: http://www.chemheritage.org/educationalservices/pharm/antibiot/readings/salt.htm.

CHEMNetBASE. "CRC Press, Periodic Table Online," Available online. URL: http://www.chemnetbase.com/periodic_table/per_table.html.

Copper Development Association. "Reclothing the First Lady of Metals," Available online. URL: http://www.copper.org/copperhome/Kids/liberty/liberty_reclothed3.html.

Emsley, John. *Nature's Building Blocks: An A-Z Guide to the Elements*. Oxford: Oxford University Press, 2001.

Encyclopedia Britannica. "Robert Wilhelm Bunsen," Available online. URL: http://www.britannica.com/eb/article-9018091/Robert-Wilhelm-Bunsen.

International Union of Pure and Applied Chemistry. "Periodic Table of the Elements," Available online. URL: http://www.iupac.org/reports/periodic_table/index.html.

Knapp, Brian. *ChemLab: Metals*. Danbury, Conn: Grolier Education, 1998.

Knapp, Brian. *Elements: Copper, Silver, and Gold*. Danbury, Conn.: Grolier Education, 1996.

———. *Science Matters: Changing Materials*. Danbury, Conn: Grolier Education, 2003.

Los Alamos National Laboratory. "Periodic Table of the Elements: A Resource for Elementary, Middle School and High School Students," Available online. URL: http://periodic.lanl. gov/default.htm.

Meiani, Antonella. *Chemistry: Experimenting with Science*. Minneapolis: Lerner Publications Co., 2003.

The National Institutes of Health's Office of Research Facilities. "Mercury Health Hazards," Available online. URL: http://orf. od.nih.gov/Environmental+Protection/Mercury+Free/ MercuryHealthHazards.htm.

National Park Service. "Statue of Liberty National Monument," Available online. URL: http://www.nps.gov/stli/historyculture/ index.htm.

Newmark, Ann. *Eyewitness Science: Chemistry*. New York: DK Publishing, 1993.

Newton, David E. *The Chemical Elements*. New York: Franklin Watts, 1994.

Nobel Prize. "Marie and Pierre Curie and the Discovery of Polonium and Radium," Available online. URL: http://nobelprize. org/nobel_prizes/physics/articles/curie/index.html.

Public Broadcasting Service (PBS). "The 'Layer Cake' Test," Available online. URL: http://www.pbs.org/wgbh/amex/bomb/ peopleevents/pandeAMEX60.html.

Rader's Chem4kids. "Metals," Available online. URL: http://www. chem4kids.com/files/elem_metal.html.

Science and Society Picture Library. "Batteries," Available online. URL: http://www.scienceandsociety.co.uk/results. asp?X9=Batteries.

Sparrow, Giles. *The Elements: Iron*. New York: Benchmark Books, 1999.

Stwertka, Albert. *A Guide to the Elements: Second Edition*. New York: Oxford University Press, 2002.

Thomas, Jens. *The Elements: Silicon*. New York: Benchmark Books, 2002.

Tillery, Bill. *Physical Science*. Columbus, Ohio: Glencoe/McGraw-Hill, 2002.

Tocci, Salvatore. *The Periodic Table*. New York: Scholastic Press, 2004.

University of College Cork Department of Chemistry. "Combustion," Available online. URL: http://www.ucc.ie/academic/chem/dolchem/html/dict/combust.html.

Watt, Susan. *The Elements: Lead*. New York: Benchmark Books, 2002.

———. *The Elements: Silver*. New York: Benchmark Books, 2003.

Woodford, Chris. *The Elements: Titanium*. New York: Benchmark Books, 2003.

World Gold Council. "Jewellery Technology," Available online. URL: http://www.gold.org/jewellery/technology/alloys/index.html?printPage=true.

FURTHER READING

Atkins, P.W. *The Periodic Kingdom: A Journey Into the Land of the Chemical Elements*. New York: Basic Books, 1995.

Cobb, Cathy and Monty L. Fetterolf. *The Joy of Chemistry: The Amazing Science of Familiar Things*. Amherst, New York: Prometheus Books, 2005.

Cobb, Cathy and Harold Goldwhite. *Creations of Fire: Chemistry's Lively History from Alchemy to the Atomic Age*. Cambridge, Mass.: Perseus Books, 2001.

Emsley, John. *Molecules at an Exhibition: Portraits of Intriguing Materials in Everyday Life*. Oxford: Oxford University Press, 1998.

Emsley, John. *Vanity, Vitality, and Virility: The Science Behind the Products You Love to Buy*. Oxford: Oxford University Press, 2004.

Gribbin, John. *The Scientists: A History of Science Told Through the Lives of Its Greatest Inventors*. New York: Random House, 2002.

Levere, Trevor H. *Transforming Matter: A History of Chemistry from Alchemy to the Buckyball*. Baltimore: Johns Hopkins University Press, 2001.

Schwarcz, Joe. *The Genie in the Bottle: 67 All-New Commentaries on the Fascinating Chemistry of Everyday Life*. New York: Henry Holt and Company, 2002.

Web Sites

American Chemical Society
www.chemistry.org/kids

This page is a special section of the Web site run by the American Chemical Society (ACS), and has a long list of easy experiments anyone can do in their own home. Using everyday household items, these experiments provide real examples of some theories and concepts in chemistry. These experiments are also available in Spanish.

Chemical Elements

www.chemicalelements.com

This Web site provides information on every element in the
periodic table of elements. Click on any square in on the table
and information on the element—mass, number, atomic structure, and more—will appear, along with additional links to
information.

Los Alamos National Laboratory, Chemistry Division

http://periodic.lanl.gov/default.htm

Featuring another periodic table of elements and resources for
elementary, middle, and high school students, this Web site is
managed by one of the most famous government laboratories
in the United States, the Los Alamos National Laboratory. Also
featured on this site are a couple of reference charts, brief expla-
nations on the basics of chemistry, and how to read the periodic
table of elements.

Rader's Chem4Kids

www.chem4kids.com

Chem4Kids is a Web site that focuses on the basics, explaining
matter, atoms, elements, and other topics as an introduction to
chemistry. It is a thorough source of information, and features
sections on the different branches of chemistry.

Web Elements

www.webelements.com

Web Elements explains the periodic table of elements, and
includes links to alternative tables, like the Janet table of elements. Each element has a Web site with a general description,
but also features more in-depth information, like nuclear, ele-
mental, and electronic properties.

PHOTO CREDITS

Page:

INDEX

ABOUT THE AUTHOR

JULIE McDOWELL is a science journalist based in Washington, D.C. She has a B.A. in journalism from Miami University in Oxford, Ohio, and a M.A. in nonfiction writing from Johns Hopkins University in Baltimore, MD. She is the coauthor of *The Lymphatic System* and author of *The Nervous System and Sense Organs*, both volumes of the Human Body Series published by Greenwood Publishing (Westport, Conn.).